THE HOUSTON DYNASTY

THE HOUSTON DYNASTY

TALES FROM COLLEGE GOLF'S GREATEST TEAM

JIM McLEAN
Foreword by Jim Nantz

RADIUS BOOK GROUP
NEW YORK

Radius Book Group
A division of Diversion Publishing Corp.
www.radiusbookgroup.com

Copyright © 2026 by Jim McLean

All rights reserved, including the right to reproduce this book or portions thereof in any form whatsoever. No part of this publication may be reproduced or transmitted in any form or by any means, electronic or mechanical, including photocopying, recording, or any other information storage and retrieval, without the written permission of the publisher.

Radius Book Group and colophon are registered trademarks of Diversion Publishing Corp.

For more information, email info@radiusbookgroup.com
First Radius Book Group Edition: March 2026

Paperback ISBN: 979-8-89515-130-3
e-ISBN: 979-8-89515-132-7

Design by Neuwirth & Associates, Inc.
Cover design by Will D. Mack

1 3 5 7 9 10 8 6 4 2

The publisher does not have any control over and does not assume any responsibility for author or third-party websites or their content.

Table of Contents

Foreword by Jim Nantz — vii
Introduction — xi

1. Welcome to Houston — 1
2. The Coach — 17
3. The Legends — 37
4. The Characters — 59
5. Life on the Links — 81
6. Tips from the Top — 93
7. You Had to Be There — 109
8. Stories I Tell at the Nineteenth Hole — 125
9. A Humbling Game — 145
10. Casualties — 167

Epilogue — 171

Foreword

In my forty years of broadcasting America's greatest championships, I've had the great honor of documenting several remarkable dynasties. The New England Patriots, the Kansas City Chiefs, and the Duke University basketball program under Coach Mike Krzyzewski, just to name a few. I could even include the dynasty that belonged to an extraordinary golfer, Tiger Woods. All of these exceptional athletes and coaches left a mark on this country's sports consciousness, and I might add that it was a thrill to broadcast so many of their iconic conquests.

I've often said that it was my good fortune to be prepared to tell these dynastic stories after witnessing greatness up close and personal when I was just a young kid attending a great university. It was at Houston where I saw and participated in a college program that was as dominant as any university sports team in American history. Sadly, it's a story that, until now, has been seldom recognized or heralded. I'm talking about the University of Houston golf team under the direction of legendary head coach Dave Williams, which won sixteen national championships in less than thirty years. For context, it was a greater success than that generation's far more acclaimed dynasty, the UCLA Men's basketball program of Coach John Wooden.

FOREWORD

It can also be said that every great dynasty deserves a storyteller—and, finally, we have the chance to learn about the legacy of the University of Houston juggernaut through my gifted friend, and one of the program's greatest contributors, Jim McLean.

Jim and I share a deep connection to the University of Houston, though our time there didn't overlap. Jim played for Coach Dave Williams almost a decade before I arrived on campus. While I was masquerading as a varsity golfer, living in a dorm with Fred Couples and Blaine McCallister, Jim had already left his mark on the team and at Houston's Baldwin House—a place where forty young, hungry golfers lived under one roof, each chasing the dream of cracking Coach Williams's top five. That dorm and that era were filled with unforgettable personalities, grueling qualifiers, and lifelong memories.

I first learned about Jim through constant glowing remarks Coach Williams reserved for one of his favorite "boys." It was an honor, a few years after school, to get to know Jim through my work with Ken Venturi at CBS. At the time, Jim was working closely with Ken, still refining his own game with the hopes of playing full-time on the PGA Tour. But it was clear, even back then, that Jim had a gift for teaching. He went on to become one of the most respected and influential golf teachers in the history of instruction. While many of the players Jim competed with went on to become stars in the PGA Tour, Jim carved out his own extraordinary path—helping build champions, mentoring hundreds of teachers, and shaping the game from the lesson tee to the major stage.

This book, *The Houston Dynasty*, focuses on the unforgettable years Jim spent as an important contributor to the golf

FOREWORD

team's dynasty. But this story reaches back into the past—and forward into the future—to tell the full story of college golf's greatest program. His insight, humor, and firsthand perspective make this more than just a memoir. It's a tribute to a golden era of college golf, to a legendary coach, and to the players who built a tradition of excellence.

If you're a fan of the game, of great coaching, or of what it means to chase something bigger than yourself, you're in for a treat. This is a story only Jim McLean could tell.

Jim Nantz,
NSMA Hall of Famer and
two-time Emmy-winning sports broadcaster

Introduction

If you've ever seen the movie *Tin Cup*, you might remember that Kevin Costner's and Don Johnson's characters were former golfers from the University of Houston. That detail wasn't just a throwaway line but a nod to reality. Houston's golf program from the 1950s to the 1980s, under legendary coach Dave Williams, produced an extraordinary number of world-class players, including major champions, Ryder Cup stars, and some of the most influential figures in the game. Even CBS's iconic Jim Nantz, who narrated the drama of *Tin Cup* as a commentator, walked the same fairways I did in Houston. That film captured the essence of what it meant to be a Houston Cougar golfer: talented, confident, and deeply believing that no stage was too big.

This book is about that dynasty: the incredible run of the Houston golf program, focusing on an amazing time from 1968 through 1972. Of course, the Houston Dynasty started before that in 1956 and lasted until 1987, a period when the Cougars dominated college golf and shaped the future of the sport. This isn't just a history lesson; it's a firsthand account of the players, the rivalries, the humor, and the madness that came with being part of something truly special. The stories in this book

INTRODUCTION

are meant to bring you inside the halls of Baldwin House, where forty golfers—yes, *forty*—lived in one hallway, in the same dorm as an NCAA powerhouse men's basketball team. It will take you inside our battles on the course, our legendary practice sessions, the betting games that could make or break your confidence, and the unforgettable characters who defined that era.

Golf has been synonymous with the University of Houston since they captured their first team national championship in 1956, a mere decade after the Cougars took to the links in 1946. Now in their eightieth year, it's hard to believe how thoroughly they dominated the sport for three decades, as evidenced by repeat conference, national, and individual championships: 1956, 1957, 1958, 1959, 1960, 1962, 1964, 1965, 1966, 1967, 1969, 1970, 1977, 1982, 1984, and 1985. During the heyday of the 1960s through the 1980s, Houston was home to a who's who of student athletes that became golf legends. The stories in this book tell the tales only those who experienced the Houston golf program know about, and even *they* only know bits and pieces. From Dave Williams to the likes of Fred Couples, Bruce Lietzke, Steve Elkington, and Billy Ray Brown, you may not believe the amazing and zany things these golfers achieved, but I assure you, everything you'll read here is true.

For me, the journey to Houston started thousands of miles away in Seattle, Washington. Growing up in the Pacific Northwest, it was hard to imagine I'd be playing golf in the Texas heat one day, let alone for the most dominant college golf program in the country. But golf has a way of shaping your path in unexpected ways.

By age sixteen, I had won the Washington State junior and the Washington State high school individual titles, and I

INTRODUCTION

played in the Western Junior at Purdue University, where I made it to the semifinals, putting my name on the radar of college coaches. The next year, I played well again at the Western Junior at Stanford, then qualified and competed well in the US Junior, proving I could hold my own against the best young players in the country. I received hundreds of letters from colleges, but then came the moment that changed everything: a call from Coach Dave Williams at the University of Houston.

Coach Williams was a legitimate legend, and Houston was by far the number one golf program in the country. I knew of the incredible players who had come through the program—tremendous players who were already making an impact on the PGA Tour. The idea of training and competing with future superstars—of being part of a program that had won so many national championships—was too big an opportunity to pass up. Coach Williams sent me dozens of letters, keeping me informed of the team's progress, and called several more times. I was sold.

Attending Houston turned out to be one of the most significant decisions of my life. Not only did I get to compete against—and alongside—some of the best players in the world, but it also shaped my future as a teacher. The lessons I learned, the techniques I absorbed, and the experiences I had with top-level golfers all played a crucial role in the success I later found as a coach.

This book is my way of sharing those stories. It's about a golden era in college golf, a team that left an indelible mark on the game, and a group of players whose names would go on to be written in golf history. It's about the camaraderie, the rivalries, the insane Texas heat, and the unforgettable moments that

INTRODUCTION

made being part of the Houston golf dynasty—to paraphrase Jim Nantz—an experience unlike any other.

For anyone who loves golf, for those who appreciate sports dynasties, and for those who just love a good story, this book is for you. It's a trip back in time to an era of pure competition, raw talent, and plenty of laughs along the way. So grab a seat, maybe a drink, and enjoy the ride. Because in the world of Houston Cougar golf, anything could—and usually did—happen.

THE HOUSTON DYNASTY

1

WELCOME TO HOUSTON

Into the Fire

I stepped off the plane in Houston, Texas, having never set foot in the Lone Star State before. It was August 17, and there was no jet bridge. For those of you born after 1980, this meant you didn't casually stroll into an air-conditioned terminal. Nope, you walked down the stairs of the plane, right into whatever weather was waiting for you. And in Houston's case, that weather was pure, unrelenting Texas heat.

The moment I hit the tarmac, it felt like I'd walked straight into an oven. Not a regular oven either, but rather one of those industrial ones used for smelting steel. It was 100 degrees with 98 percent humidity, and that humidity hit me like a wet wool blanket soaked in boiling water. Coming from the cool, damp Northwest, I'd never felt anything like it. My first thought? *How do people live here?* My second thought? *I might not make it to baggage claim.*

Now the Texas folks on the plane with me? Completely unfazed. They walked off the plane like they were stepping into a mild spring day. One of them even said, "Little warm today, huh?" like it wasn't hot enough to fry an egg on the wing of the plane. I was convinced I'd landed on another planet.

Meanwhile, I'm melting. My shirt is plastered to my back, and my lungs are desperately trying to figure out how to breathe.

My total luggage included one small suitcase and my golf bag. That's it. I had never visited the city before, and to top it off, I didn't even have a ride to campus. I got a cab and prayed the driver knew where Baldwin House was located at the University of Houston.

The cab ride from Hobby Airport (this was before Houston George Bush International) was an adventure of its own. The driver, wearing a cowboy hat, played old-time country music the whole ride. He didn't say a word the entire time, unless you count the occasional grunt when he turned the wheel. The AC was barely working, so I sat there in my own private sauna, staring out at a city that seemed to stretch on forever.

When we finally pulled up to Baldwin House, I dragged my belongings inside and checked in. Baldwin House was no Ritz-Carlton, let me tell you. It was a sturdy, 1960s dorm—functional, sure, but about as glamorous as a high school locker room. The second-floor hallway would be my new home, where "home" meant cinder block walls and fluorescent lights.

I climbed the stairs, dripping sweat, and made my way to my room centered in the hallway. My roommate was Bruce Ashworth, who was my opponent from our US Junior encounter and my teammate, along with another Houston sophomore, Bobby Walzel, in the Western Junior at Stanford that past July.

Bruce was already a solid player through and through—relaxed and confident. He was from Las Vegas and very accustomed to healthy golf betting. He greeted me with a grin, a firm handshake, and a casual "Man, it's a little sticky out today, huh?" Sticky. That's what he called it. *Sticky.*

Our room was basic: two sections with a bathroom in between. Nothing fancy, but it worked. Next door to us were two of the top juniors in America: Jim Simons, who had already qualified for the US Open (yes, *the* US Open), and Mike Killian, the top-ranked junior golfer from Florida. Just what I expected.

It didn't take long for me to realize I was stepping into a world where nobody cared about your junior record or how many trophies you had back home. At Houston, everyone was a star—until they weren't. You started at the bottom, and if you wanted to climb, you had to prove yourself. Coach Williams made sure of that.

But at that moment, I wasn't thinking about proving myself. I was thinking about how I'd survive this heat, unpack my luggage, and maybe, just maybe, figure out how to breathe again.

Welcome to Houston. Where the heat hits you harder than a linebacker blitzing through the screen door.

Initiation

When I first arrived at the University of Houston, I quickly learned that initiation was not for the faint of heart—or hair. The ritual started with a clean buzz cut for every freshman golfer. Yep, every last one of us in Baldwin House ended up bald as a cue ball. There we were, a whole row of freshmen with freshly shaved heads, looking like a bunch of mismatched eggs. You'd think they were prepping us for basic training, not for a golf team.

My freshman year was the last of the "true" Houston Cougar golf team initiations. Until my year, which would be the last, Coach Williams and the upperclassmen took initiation as seriously as they took our scores, and, boy, it was something you'd never forget. Freshmen were nobodies back then, banned from varsity play for all college sports. We had our own freshman team, but it wasn't exactly front-page news. Basically, we were zeros—walking practice dummies for the upperclassmen.

Once our heads were shaved, they made us tie these ridiculous plastic balls on top of our heads with a ribbon that we had to wear each day to class. It was like some sadistic birthday party favor. We looked like bald little aliens with antennae, bobbing around campus. As if that wasn't enough, some days they'd slap sandwich boards over us, with messages like "Go Cougars" on one side and "NCAA Champions" on the other. Real subtle. But word spread quickly, and everyone on campus knew exactly who we were—and they stayed a good six feet away from us.

Evenings were often for shoe duty. If you were unlucky, you were chosen to scrub the upperclassmen's shoes till they sparkled like diamonds, digging out every last speck of that stubborn Texas clay. If those shoes weren't gleaming enough to blind you, well, you'd be scrubbing again. My roommate Bruce, bless his heart, usually kept me safe and hidden. Then came the shag bags. Now I doubt anyone even knows what a shag bag is anymore but, back then, it was just a bag full of practice balls. You see, range balls weren't part of golf, and most ranges were just fields. That's where golfers hit shag balls and then picked them up themselves. That's exactly what he did for our practice. Obviously, we cleaned the upperclassmen's shag balls in the evenings too.

Then there were the Quick Stop runs. If you were lucky, they didn't wake *you* up for one of these. At around 1 or 2 a.m., you'd get a rough nudge from an upperclassman, mumbling, "Run down to Quick Stop and get me some chips. And a six-pack of tall boys." That, my friend, was a mission you didn't argue with.

We were all very aware initiation night would be a no-holds-barred event. Everyone kept a tight lid on the details though, which only made us more uptight. Finally initiation night arrived, and they rounded us all up in Baldwin House and stripped us down to our underwear. First came the paddling, naturally. We'd grab our ankles, and the upperclassmen would let us have it. Then you had to say, "Thank you, sir. Can I have another?" Younger readers are probably thinking this was some medieval torture ritual, but back then, it was just another college initiation, common at most fraternities.

Then it was up to the roof, where the real *games* began. We were blindfolded and leaned over a toilet full of squishy, foul-smelling bananas, and we had to squeeze 'em with our hands. Of course, we all thought it was something far worse. I still remember an upperclassman shouting, "Oh, Lord, it's a fresh one!" We ran these ridiculous races with our butts barely an inch off the ground and got put through a series of stunts that tested our ability to grin and bear it. Initiation night lasted a good two hours, and there were a few other frightening ordeals that are better left out.

Looking back, yeah, those initiations were archaic. And that was the last year they did them. But you know what? Nobody got hurt and, somehow, we all made it through. Sure, there was a lot of mumbling, but we walked away feeling like we'd survived something that definitely bonded us.

The one thing they didn't make us do—thank God—was the legendary bayou night swim. Now this was whispered about in the week leading up to initiation. The rumor was that they'd make us swim across the bayou near the school, which might sound easy enough until you consider the hundreds of water moccasins and who-knows-what-else slithering through that water. No bayou swim? Well, that was one part of initiation we didn't miss one bit.

Baldwin House: The Golfer's Hall

If you've ever wondered what happens when you put forty college golfers into one hallway of an athletic dorm, let me paint you a picture: Baldwin House at the University of Houston, 1968. The hallway was more than where we lived and moved from room to room—it was our driving range, our putting green, and, occasionally, a battlefield. You had to be careful coming out of your room because someone could be lacing a 1-iron down the hallway. The entry doors on both sides of the hall? Solid steel but covered in a million dents. Not just little dings, mind you. I'm talking exact golf-ball-sized craters, each a perfect circle from teammates ripping shots down the corridor. Baldwin House wasn't just our dorm, but also a hazard zone.

We shared the dorm with the UH basketball team, who were no strangers to fame themselves. Just the year before, they'd gone 35–0 and made it to the NCAA tournament, only to lose to

WELCOME TO HOUSTON

UCLA in the semifinals. This was the same Houston team that had beaten UCLA earlier in the year at the famous Astrodome game, with seventy thousand people watching, which is still the record for a basketball crowd. I might add this was an additional recruiting tool. Since I loved basketball and was a starting guard on my high school team, I was riveted to the TV, watching that Houston game against UCLA.

But back to the golf team. It's 1968, and we're coming off yet another NCAA Championship—winning was what the University of Houston golf team did, and Coach Williams made sure of that. When he recruited me the year before, he didn't just tell me the Houston golf team had won the past two NCAA Championships in a row. He predicted we would win the next four. He *expected* me to be part of the next one. Coach didn't recruit players—he wanted to recruit winners. And with forty guys on the team, it was assured that five could really play.

Living in Baldwin House meant you were more than just part of a team. You were part of a dynasty. By the time I graduated, we had won twelve of the past sixteen NCAA Championships and finished second in the other four. That wasn't luck. That was life under Coach Williams. He turned Houston golf into a juggernaut, and we all knew it.

But Baldwin House wasn't exactly living in luxury. Sharing a hallway with forty golfers meant chaos was the norm. Golf balls flying down the hall was just part of daily life. Forget looking both ways before crossing the street—you learned to look both ways before stepping out of your room. Nobody wanted to get nailed by a 1-iron, but if you did, it would be because you were a dumbass. And, trust me, nobody was going to be the first one carried out on a stretcher with a ball embedded in their back.

Then there were the personalities. I was surrounded by future legends—guys who would go on to win the Masters, the US Open, the British Open, and the PGA Championship. Walker Cup members and Ryder Cup members and future Hall of Fame members. But back then, we were just a bunch of young guys trying to one-up each other, on and off the course. You'd think that kind of talent might make things super serious, but nope. It was pure Texas-style, with a side of future world-class golf.

And Coach Williams? He was the ringmaster. Coach had a way of making us believe we were invincible. He did more than recruit talent—he built it. He'd find a kid from the middle of nowhere, hand him a Houston golf bag, and turn him into an NCAA Champion. The man was a genius—and tough too.

Baldwin House was where it all came together. Sure, we sometimes made a mess of the place, and I'm pretty sure the dents in those steel doors are still there. But it wasn't only a hallway. It was a proving ground, a clubhouse, and a second home.

Looking back, it's funny how much we packed into one hallway. And yet, out of that chaos came a boatload of top players. Baldwin House may have been where we lived, but it was also where we became a real team and serious competitors.

Don Scott vs. The Texas Ant Army

If you've spent more than five minutes in Texas, you've probably encountered red ants. But these aren't your average ants—they're the Navy SEALs of the insect world. Vicious, strategic, and always looking for an excuse to ruin your day. Step on a red ant hill, you have just struck a declaration of war.

WELCOME TO HOUSTON

During my time in Texas, I had plenty of run-ins with these demons. Sometimes it was my fault—I'd lean a hand on the wrong tree or set a headcover on the ground without a thought. Big mistake. A *Texas-sized mistake*. The ants would swarm like they'd been training their entire lives for that moment.

But nothing—*nothing*—compared to what happened to Don Scott during my first month in Texas. It was the Houston City Amateur, a big local event. Don was a talented player from the Pacific Northwest, known for his smooth swing and slightly naive disposition. He wasn't on the traveling team often, but that week, at Hermann Park Golf Course, he was dialed in. By the third round, standing on the fifty-fourth hole, Don still had a slim lead.

Then disaster struck.

Don hit his second shot on par five just barely into a water hazard, about eighty yards short of the 18th green. Now this wasn't one of those pristine, perfectly manicured hazards you see at your local private club. Oh, no. This was Texas, where hazards were untamed jungles of high grass, thorns, vines, and god knows what else. A creek weaved through it, surrounded by brush, and the red line marking the hazard was just outside the non-maintained areas.

Don, determined to save his round, found his ball about three yards in the high grass. We watched from the clubhouse patio, sipping Dr Peppers and munching on burgers, as he carefully walked into the hazard. He assessed the shot, stared at the green for a few seconds, and made a few practice waggles, careful to not ground his club. And then, suddenly, like a scene out of a horror movie, it happened.

The ants struck.

At first, there was nothing. Don, standing in the brush, looked calm and focused. But unbeknownst to him, a battalion of red ants had begun their silent invasion. They scaled his shoes, then his socks, then his legs. These ants were tactical geniuses—they didn't bite immediately. Oh, no. They waited until their entire army was in position, like tiny, coordinated paratroopers. And then, all at once, they attacked.

One second, Don was about to take his shot. The next, he was airborne, flailing his arms and legs like he was drowning in Lake Houston. His screams echoed across the course as he ran in circles, swatting these very nasty soldiers. To us, safely watching from the clubhouse, it looked like he was trying to fight off an angry poltergeist.

He stumbled out of the hazard, his face twisted in agony. The ants had gone to work, and these weren't the kind of bites you just brush off. No, these were Texas red ant bites, which feel like molten lava being injected directly into your soul. And the ants don't let go either. Once their pincers are in, it's a full-on tug-of-war to remove them. Don was now on the ground, trying to brush them off. It was brutal to watch, and the next thing we saw, Don was put into a golf cart and was off to the hospital. His legs looked like they'd been used for target practice by a swarm of angry archers. Rumor has it that, on the ride over, he managed to mutter, "Did I save par?" before slipping into pain-induced delirium. He didn't win the tournament that day, and he didn't make it for the fourth round, but he did leave Hermann Park Golf Course with a new title: *The Man Who Went Toe-to-Toe with the Texas Ant Army . . . and Lost.*

The whole ordeal left us shaken. It was like watching a golf horror story unfold in real time. As the medics rolled Don away,

Coach gathered us together for a little pep talk. "Gentlemen," he said, "lesson of the day: No ball is worth dying for. If you see ants, drop, take the penalty, and walk away. Forget the ball—it's theirs now."

From that day forward, I became one of the *more cautious* golfers in Texas. Before stepping into any hazard, I'd do a full, military-style reconnaissance mission. I'd poke the ground with a club, wait for movement, and if I saw so much as a single ant, I'd back away like the area was rigged with explosives.

The thing about Texas ants is they don't just ruin your day—they change your whole outlook on life. They're a force of nature; a reminder that, in the grand scheme of things, humans aren't in charge here. You think you're tough because you can hit a three-hundred-yard drive? Please. Texas ants will humble you faster than a shank off the first tee.

So if you're ever golfing in Texas, let me give you some advice: Forget about the snakes, the gators, and even the cactus needles. It's the ants you've got to watch out for. Because when those little red demons show up, there are only two outcomes: You're leaving the course on your own two feet . . . or on a stretcher, questioning every life choice that brought you to that moment.

And if you're still thinking, *It's just ants, how bad can it be?* Well, my friend, you've clearly never been to Texas.

A Summer of Sweat, Swings, and Survival

As my freshman year at the University of Houston wrapped up, I found myself summoned to the office of the great and powerful

Coach Dave Williams. When Coach asked you to sit down for a chat, it wasn't to discuss your favorite breakfast cereal.

He got straight to the point. "Jim, I want you back next year, but you better improve your game."

It was like being told by a doctor, "You'll live, but we might have to amputate your left arm." I nodded, shook his hand, and walked out of his office, pretending I had everything under control. The truth? I had spent most of my freshman year playing golf—not very well—and then watching fifteen of the seventeen freshmen around me either transfer or vanish into the abyss. Houston golf was the definition of survival of the fittest, and based on my performance, I was somewhere between a wounded gazelle and a three-legged coyote.

Thankfully, I had my best college buddy, Jim Simons, to keep me company during that year. We played many rounds, practiced together, and survived freshman year together, and we had some fun along the way. But Jim, unfortunately, did not even make it to the last week of our first year—he was kicked off the team. (More on that later.)

Of course, Jim went on to become one of the greatest amateurs in history when he nearly won the 1971 US Open. But in 1968, we were just two promising players who were definitely fearing the upperclassmen.

Coach had made himself clear: I needed to get a lot better, and fast. He had expected more. He had invested a four-year scholarship on me. The heat was on.

When I got back home to Seattle for the summer, my dad had a different plan for me.

"You're going to be working a job," he said, without a hint of negotiation in his voice. "You'll be loading chairs onto trains."

Well, that sounded . . . not good.

"You know I have to get better at golf," I told him. "Coach Williams made that very clear. I need serious practice time, Dad." I hoped he'd see the flaw in his master plan.

"Yeah, your shift is from 7 a.m. to 2 p.m.," he replied. "Plenty of time to practice after that. It doesn't get dark until 9."

Ah, yes. Plenty of time to practice—after seven tough hours of moving what felt like a small nation's worth of awkwardly shaped chairs onto a train car that sat on tracks running from Seattle all the way back East and all over America.

By the end of each shift, my arms felt like they had personally lost a fight. It definitely was not helping the practice I knew I needed.

I was still an eighteen-year-old college kid, which meant I also had an obligation to go out at night with all my old Seattle buddies. That meant I was running on fumes—working all morning, dragging myself to the golf course in the afternoon, and then heading out many nights, only to do it all over again the next day.

After about a month of this routine, I sat my dad down for a serious talk.

"Dad, I want to practice all day, every day," I told him, trying to sound as professional as possible. "I can't do that if I'm spending half my time stacking chairs."

To my complete shock, he agreed. He realized that, since my four-year scholarship covered everything, and I was getting an additional six-hundred-dollar monthly stipend, I was essentially paying my own way through school. He let me quit the job, and just like that, I transitioned from a semi-professional furniture mover to a full-time golfer.

With no more physical labor slowing me down, I threw myself into golf like never before. I practiced sunup to sundown, hitting thousands of golf balls, and something miraculous happened: I started regaining lost confidence and began shooting low scores again.

The first sign of progress? I won my club championship. Now was this like winning a big tournament? No. But for a guy who had spent the previous year getting steamrolled by Houston's varsity players, it was proof that I might be heading in the right direction.

Then I won the Pacific Northwest Amateur held that year in Vancouver, British Columbia. This was the biggest amateur tournament in the Northwest. It first meant qualifying for match play—I was the medalist shooting 139, then I was winning six matches and playing singles against the best players from the West Coast and British Columbia. (The semifinals and finals were thirty-six holes.) In later years, a young guy named Tiger Woods would also win this event, and when he did, everyone saw it as a sign of his inevitable greatness. When I won, my parents, and especially me, were just relieved that I wouldn't have to go back to loading trains.

Returning to Houston that fall, I wasn't the same guy who had stumbled through freshman year. I had a newfound confidence in my game and, more importantly, actual proof that I could compete. I wasn't just showing up to qualifiers—I was contending.

I competed hard through the fall, getting closer to making the top five. And finally, it paid off. In the spring, I qualified for my first big college tournament: the Arizona State Thunderbird Invitational in Tucson, where many of the top college teams in America were playing.

WELCOME TO HOUSTON

This was it—my introduction to the Houston travel team and real competitive college golf. Sure, I had spent part of the past summer hauling stacks of chairs, but I was finally where I wanted to be: competing against the best.

And you know what? Coach's motivational talk had worked. I had, in fact, gotten better. But I didn't tell him the real reason for my success: not lifting chairs in a Seattle warehouse.

2

THE COACH

The Origins of Dave Williams, Golf Coach Extraordinaire

Growing up in the small town of Randolph, Texas, Coach Dave Williams was an all-around athlete, dabbling in every sport he could find. He wasn't *the* star of Randolph, but he was good enough to earn a spot in the constellation—let's call him a "medium star." While his talent on the sports fields was evident, his true passion wasn't scoring touchdowns or hitting home runs. What Dave really wanted was to coach. Even as a boy, he declared to his brothers, Noble and Clovis, that he would one day become a coach—*the* coach. In fact, he wanted to be the next Bear Bryant.

Born on October 14, 1918, his parents named him Glenwood Williams, but at some point, an uncle stepped in and suggested they upgrade the name to David G. Williams, which had a sturdier, more coach-like ring to it.

Growing up in Randolph wasn't easy. Coach worked the cotton fields, chopping for one dollar a day—a fortune if you ignore the grueling labor. Dave liked to brag that he held the town record for the most cotton chopped in one day: a whopping 579 pounds. (Whether anyone kept official records is questionable, but when you're chopping cotton, exaggeration is earned.)

In 1939, Dave graduated from East Texas State University and became a teacher, lured by a salary that seemed princely at the time. "I made $1,100 my first year out of college," he told *Sports Illustrated* in 1984. "That was *money*. I went straight to Dallas, bought a car, and the first three suits I'd ever owned." By comparison, the local postman made sixty-four dollars a month—Coach's paycheck was so desirable, he joked, "[I] could've married anyone in Hunt County."

During World War II, Coach attended the Naval Academy, where he earned master's degrees in engineering and chemistry. By 1946, he landed a teaching job at the University of Houston. However, academics alone weren't enough to satisfy the itch for competition that had followed him since childhood. That's when he enlisted his brothers, Noble and Clovis, in a search for a new TV athletic outlet.

"I said to Noble, 'We can't play football or basketball anymore, but we've been in sports all our lives. We *have* to find something,'" Coach recalled. The brothers dug up a dusty set of old golf clubs from Clovis's garage, and just like that, a new obsession was born.

Golf was entirely foreign to Dave. He didn't even know where to find golf balls, eventually spotting some at an auto supply store for two dollars a dozen. "No telling what kind they were," he said. Armed with their bargain balls and mismatched clubs, the brothers headed to Glenbrook Municipal Golf Course, a hazard-filled labyrinth of creeks and canals. Predictably, their golf balls didn't last long, sinking to watery graves faster than they could swing. Noble gave up, but Dave was hooked. He began waking up early to play at Glenbrook, hacking his way around the course until it was time to teach his first class at 11 a.m.

His dedication eventually paid off: Coach broke one hundred for eighteen holes, a personal milestone that fueled his passion. He found a playing partner in Harry Fouke, the athletic director at the University of Houston. Harry introduced him to two other coaches, and the foursome often played friendly wagers that Coach consistently lost. But as his game improved, he started turning the tables. One day, he shot a seventy-four and won. The next day, another seventy-four. Harry, impressed by Coach's athletic insight and persistence, had an idea.

"You want to coach golf?" Harry asked.

"What do I have to do?" Coach replied.

"Just pass out some balls and tell the boys to get after it," Harry said.

And just like that, in 1951, Coach Dave Williams became the head golf coach at the University of Houston. The program was a mess, with a twenty-five-match losing streak and only two partial scholarships to its name. Coach wasn't even paid for the role—it was strictly volunteer. But Dave, ever the optimist, took the job with gusto.

Houston had one match left that season, against Lamar Tech. Harry suggested they play behind the team, as was custom, but Coach refused. "If I'm going to be their coach, I'm going to watch them play," he said. His team won, snapping the losing streak.

THE HOUSTON DYNASTY

"It was an accident," Coach would later say. "I didn't say a word. But I was there, and they won. And I remember every single shot those boys hit that day. They were my people."

At that year's spring sports banquet, Coach was asked to give a speech. He was nervous so he blurted out the first thing that came to mind: "The University of Houston golf team is going to win the national championship!" The room erupted in laughter. His team wasn't even *in* the NCAA. From that day on, people started calling him "National Championship Williams."

And wouldn't you know it, by 1956, the Houston Cougars did exactly what "National Championship Williams" had promised: They claimed their first NCAA title. But that was only the beginning. With Coach at the helm, the team went on to win NCAA championships in 1957, 1958, 1959, and 1960, making it look like Houston was building a dynasty on pure grit, Texas swagger, and Coach's unbreakable belief that they could be the best. He turned the Cougar golf team from a scrappy operation into a national powerhouse.

But Coach was just getting warmed up. After taking a brief pause from the championship spotlight, his Cougars claimed the title again in 1962, then from 1964 to 1967. By now, Houston was the talk of college golf, and Coach was becoming something of a legend himself. To celebrate his string of victories, the university built a trophy room dedicated solely to the golf team's ever-growing haul of hardware. Those glittering trophies were more than decorations—they were a promise of the program's excellence, a gleaming testament to Coach's relentless vision.

It didn't stop there. With a steady hand and unwavering faith in his recruits, Coach kept Houston on top. The Cougars grabbed NCAA titles again in 1969 and 1970, capping a decade where they utterly dominated college golf. Coach wanted to make Houston *the* destination for anyone serious about the sport, and under his leadership, they not only won twelve national championships in two decades, but consistently turned out golfers who would go on to make waves on the PGA Tour.

Houston was obviously the team to beat, and though they fell just short, finishing as runners-up in both 1971 and 1972, Coach's influence was undeniable. Houston's rivals knew they weren't just competing against a team—they were facing off against a legacy that Coach had built from the ground up, one sweat-drenched swing and handwritten letter at a time.

Coach's recruiting technique was as unique as he was. With no budget for cross-country visits, he didn't travel to meet recruits in person, shake hands with their parents, or promise four-year scholarships like the big-name schools did. Instead, he relied on a blizzard of letters and relentless phone calls. Recruits received stacks of letters, each one marked with Coach's unmistakable, handwritten corrections. His phone calls were constant, personal, and persuasive. He'd pitch players on a vision: "Come to Houston, win a championship, and make history." The trophies spoke for themselves, and so did the roster of Cougar alumni climbing the PGA ranks, with players who'd tasted college championships under Coach and went on to make names for themselves as PGA Tour professionals.

But Coach wasn't satisfied with past victories. He was determined to keep Houston on top and solidify his legacy. I was one of those recruits when Coach made an unprecedented move: offering a full scholarship to a talented young player from the Pacific Northwest. Before this, Coach would never offer a four-year scholarship, but now other schools were doing this consistently, and the competition was on. I told him I had a four-year scholarship offer from two top competitors, Stanford and Arizona State, plus from many other schools. With that, Coach's recruiting tactics evolved from humble handwritten letters and six-month scholarships to competitive, multiyear scholarship offers so he could maintain Houston as a destination for elite golfers. But it wouldn't be long before the forty-player squads would be pared down. Players would no longer stay on campus in the dorms. That would change. I, however, would experience the entire Houston golf team experience, undergoing the whole enchilada.

By the time the dust settled, Coach had accomplished more than most coaches could dream of. His Cougars collected seventeen NCAA titles under his leadership, a feat that cemented both his name and the University of Houston in golf history. What started as a one-man experiment, with borrowed clubs and discount balls, turned into a college golf dynasty that transformed the landscape of the sport. And through it all, Coach remained true to his roots: a Texas original with a vision and an uncanny knack for turning grit and determination into championships.

Years later, as people looked back at his career, the trophies filling Houston's hallways are more than symbols of victory. They are living proof of Dave Williams's legacy: a coach who never settled for anything less than greatness, even when the world thought he was crazy for daring to dream that big.

Dave Williams was a visionary, a recruiter, and a builder of champions. His medium-star youth had given way to a legacy that would shine brightly for generations to come. Plain and simple: He built the Houston Dynasty.

THE COACH

Lost in America and Coach Williams's Famous Team Meetings

Coach Williams would launch into his long speeches, jumping from life advice to tournament tactics and back again, never once venturing into swing mechanics. He was famously hands-off about the technical side, but he knew how to mold a team, which was all that mattered to him.

Part of Coach's charm—or chaos, depending on who you asked—was his valiant yet never-quite-successful attempt to remember everyone's name. With forty-odd guys on the roster, it was like trying to memorize the Houston phone book. But Coach had a workaround: He'd skip the name and go straight for the hometown. "Dallas, you're up next!" he'd shout across the range, nodding toward a bewildered freshman who had no choice but to play along. If he couldn't remember where you were from, he'd default to a vague "Texas!" which conveniently applied to half the team.

Over time, most of us stopped correcting him. He'd look around the room, eyes narrowing as he tried to connect faces with cities. "New Orleans, New Orleans, you're with F Troop playing at Texaco CC this week." You'd answer with all the conviction you could muster, hoping he wouldn't call you "Louisiana" next time.

Occasionally, though, things got mixed up. "Chicago!" he'd bark, only to have three guys from Illinois look up, wondering who he meant. Or he'd point to someone from Tennessee and accidentally call them "Georgia" because, in his mind, they were close enough.

The older players found it endlessly amusing, having learned to play along and accept whatever moniker he assigned. But for the freshmen, it was an initiation of sorts. Each newbie had to brace themselves for the day when Coach would rename them on a whim. A kid from Albuquerque became "Arizona" for an entire season. One guy from North Dakota was dubbed "Canada," and after a while, even he stopped trying to correct it.

When you had a coach like Dave Williams, who called on cities and states rather than people, the team meetings had their own peculiar rhythm. He'd quiz "Dallas" about bunkers, scold "San Antonio" for showing up late, and commend "Mississippi" for an imaginary improvement in driving distance. It was like living in a map that only he could read.

The Legendary All-American Golf Tournament of 1969

When it comes to college golf, no name stands taller than Coach Dave Williams. He was the architect of a dynasty so dominant, it's hard to even comprehend today. Coach led the University of Houston golf program to an unfathomable seventeen NCAA Championships—a record so untouchable, it looks like it is built to last for eternity. Seventeen titles: Think about it. Nobody's even close. It's not just a record but a legacy carved in stone.

But Coach's brilliance went far beyond the golf course. He was a master recruiter, promoter, and showman—qualities that came together perfectly in the All-American Intercollegiate Golf Tournament, which is an event he personally dreamed up, developed, and ran with unmatched flair. By 1969, the tournament had become *the* event in college golf—unrivaled, electric, and pure Dave Williams genius. I know because I was a freshman that year, wide-eyed at everything I was witnessing.

To call the All-American a "golf tournament" doesn't do it justice. It was part championship, part Texas-style spectacle, and all Dave Williams. Nobody in college golf was putting on a show like this: The 1969 edition had an attendance of ten thousand spectators—a staggering number for a college event. There were also beverages to purchase, just like at a PGA Tour event. Coach understood that golf could draw a crowd, but only if you gave them something special. You had to put on a show!

And, oh, did he know how to put on a show.

For starters, there was the Golf Queen Contest: an all-campus event where one lucky female student was crowned the All-American Queen. This was no rinky-dink title since the winner received a watch and a *brand-new car*—well, a car for the rest of the year. But for a college student, that was about as good as it got. She was honored in front of over five hundred people at the All-American Banquet the night prior to the tournament's first round. Picture all the teams, coaches, players, and the University of Houston's own Queen at the center of it all, smiling like she just won the lottery. And the pomp didn't stop there.

Coach understood that an event was about more than its competition. It was also about experience. To make visiting teams feel special—and probably to sneakily woo their best players—Coach ensured every team got their own slice of Houston hospitality. Each university captain, in front of the crowd, had the honor of choosing two beautiful female hosts for the week. These ladies were ambassadors, blending Texas charm with the warmth of the University of Houston. This wasn't just a logistical courtesy but rather a spectacle in itself and one of the tournament's most anticipated moments.

For the teams and coaches, it was the perfect mix of fun, focus, and a reminder that Houston was *the place* to be for college golf.

Then there was the music. The University of Houston Band—in full uniform, no less—played the fight song for *every single team* that attended the tournament. This might seem small on paper, but imagine the effect: players from Oklahoma, Texas, Florida, and beyond hearing their school pride ring out across the course. It made every team feel like they were playing for something bigger, like they were a part of a historic occasion.

Of course, none of this was accidental. Coach was always a step ahead. He ran the All-American Tournament, not only as a championship, but as a recruiting tool. He understood that if he brought the best players in the country to Houston, they'd see something they couldn't find anywhere else. The massive crowds, the over-the-top banquet, the local support, the prestige—it was all part of the pitch. It was more than beating other schools to Coach. He wanted the future stars of golf to choose Houston, and it worked.

Coach was a master builder, turning events like this into cornerstones of his program's success.

As a freshman in 1968, I was aware the program would be special. I knew about Houston's golf dominance, and I knew I was joining the top-ranked team in the nation. That's why I went there. But the All-American Tournament? That was something else entirely. The crowds, the music, the Golf Queen contest—it was more like a festival than a golf tournament. It felt like every detail was designed to show off the University of Houston as *the* place to be.

For the Houston players, the event was the number one tournament of the year, and the pressure was real. Coach expected success, and he built the environment to ensure it. The golf world was watching, and we were wearing Houston's red and white. Whether you were a seasoned upperclassman or a clueless freshman like me, you knew you were part of something historic.

Looking back, the 1969 All-American Tournament—held during the spring semester—perfectly encapsulates what made Dave Williams such a legend. He wasn't content with winning titles; instead, he wanted to make college golf bigger, better, and bolder than anyone thought possible. And he did.

The All-American was a statement. It was Coach saying, "This is Houston. This is where the best play. Come see for yourself."

And for ten thousand fans, thirty-two Houston Honeys, dozens of teams, and one lucky Golf Queen, 1969 was proof that Dave Williams was the undisputed king of college golf.

Winning the All-American

So whenever you think about the greatest college golf tournaments ever, you have to put the All-American at the top of the list. At least that's how Coach wanted it. The All-American was the biggest college event outside of the NCAA Championship.

To get a sense of the magnitude, the final round was televised, and we had ten thousand people crowding the course to watch the action unfold. It was Houston's version of the Masters, with a Texas twist: Coach had personally sold sponsorships to every Houston business that would listen, charged admission fees, and made it a full-blown spectacle. The tournament kicked off with a high-profile banquet featuring famous speakers, two NFL quarterbacks, and even a few politicians thrown in for good measure. This was the last time the tournament was held at Pine Forest Golf Club, not far from downtown Houston, and it would never be this big again.

For the Houston players who weren't competing, Coach made sure there was no time to sit back and watch the show. Everyone had a job. Freshmen, of course, got the remedial tasks. For me, that meant caddying for my roommate Bruce Ashworth. I hadn't caddied since I was twelve but, compared to some of the other grunt work, I considered myself very lucky. At least I wasn't manning the scoreboard in the Texas sun, or polishing shoes in the clubhouse, or picking up the trash like some of the other rookies. Pine Forest Golf Club was our battleground that year, with every top team in America attending and, most importantly, with Houston and the University of Texas squaring off in a showdown as intense as any rivalry could get. As usual, Texas had a powerhouse team, and every shot ratcheted up the tension a notch higher.

In 1969, it all came down to the final hole. Houston held a one-shot lead over Texas, and there we were on the eighteenth hole, with the weight of the tournament on our shoulders. Bruce missed the green, landing in the rough to the left. My pulse raced as he walked over to his ball, knowing that every eye in the gallery was locked onto him. The tournament could easily go either way now. But then, with the calm precision of a surgeon, Bruce pitched it to within a foot of the cup, sealing the tournament for Houston. I'll never forget the roar from the gallery that day. It was an unforgettable moment—my first taste of high-stakes college golf. Caddying all seventy-two holes was a trial by fire and a crash course in pressure, patience, and the weight of competition.

But, as any college freshman knows, the "real" experience usually starts after a big event ends.

The victory party that night was everything you'd expect from a team of forty college guys who'd just beaten their biggest rival on the biggest stage. We celebrated like we'd won the Masters, the Super Bowl, and the World Series all at once. Drinks were flowing, laughter was booming, and I . . . Well, let's just say I might have taken the celebration a little too seriously.

By the end of the night, I was in no condition to do much of anything, let alone handle the delicate task of removing my contact lenses. Bruce took one look at me when I stumbled into our dorm room, shook his head, and stepped in to save the day—or, more accurately, my eyes. While I swayed and slurred, he gingerly removed my contacts, muttering something about this being his pay for the caddying job. Somehow, my teammates got me into bed, where I promptly went out like a light.

The next day, I woke up feeling like I'd been run over by a truck, dragged halfway to Austin, and then run over again. My head was pounding, my stomach was in revolt, and moving was out of the question. Bruce practically carried me over to the university hospital, where doctors took one look at me and delivered the kind of sigh reserved for freshmen who'd taken their first victory celebration way too far. Apparently, I'd narrowly avoided dying from alcohol poisoning. A classic freshman blunder, they called it—one of those "live and learn" lessons you never forget.

And that, in a nutshell, was my story of the 1969 All-American: the high of winning on the course and the low of being wheeled into UH Medical the next morning.

Tucson

I finally made the team as a sophomore, after yet another grueling eight-round qualifier. I'd been close so many times, and now, near the end of the season, I finally cracked through. Coach was still deciding who he would take to the upcoming NCAA Championship. He was solid on the first four players, but that fifth spot was still up for grabs. And one of the most surprising things? Our first-team All-American John Mahaffey, a great player, had been in a long slump. There was a good chance that John wouldn't go to the NCAA, which cracked the door open for me.

So off we flew to Tucson for the Sun Devil Classic. All the top teams were there—the West Coast heavyweights like USC, UCLA, Arizona State, and the University of Arizona, plus our rivals from Texas, Oklahoma State, and Wake Forest. It was going to be a test, with the first round set for twenty-seven holes and another twenty-seven the next day. We'd then fly back to Houston that night to avoid missing another day of classes.

Things started out well enough. I shot an excellent 3-under on the front nine, bringing my score to 33. I was feeling confident, riding high on a wave of pars and birdies, but then I hit the back nine, and the wheels started wobbling. The eighteenth hole at Tucson was one of those par-4s that separated the men from the boys—a notorious water hazard waiting to devour any shot that strayed even a hair off-target on either side. I managed to contribute to the eighteenth's reputation by sending one into the drink and scrambling my way to a double-bogey 6. That turned my 33 into 40 on the back, bringing my score to 73 total. A respectable score, but I was shaken from that poor finish.

Now there's no leisurely lunch at these tournaments. You grab a quick bite and you're back on the course. But something went very wrong in that third nine: I found myself on the dreaded bogey train as a desert wind blew in. Bogey after bogey, I couldn't make a par to save my life. I'd thrown in a double for good measure and walked up to the eighteenth green in the dark, carding one of the highest nine-hole scores of my life, at least since age thirteen.

Coach was waiting up on the hill with the rest of the team as I finished. He called out, "What'd you shoot?"

All I could do was own it. "Forty-five," I said, bracing for impact.

He looked at me, arms crossed, eyebrows raised, and then let out a heavy sigh. But the kicker? John Mills, another teammate and a future first-team All-American, had just come in with a 44. These were unheard-of scores for the University of Houston—practically a sin.

Coach didn't say a word. He just fell back on the grass, put his arms behind his head, closed his eyes, and didn't move. I mean no movement. For a good ten minutes, we thought he might have had a heart attack. His face was ashen white, and he was literally frozen to the ground. I thought I might've finished his career! No one dared disturb him, knowing he'd finally reached his breaking point. We were now in third place.

Dinner that night was a solemn affair, with Coach in a totally depressed mood as he ate in silence. At least he wasn't dead.

The next day, I managed to play better, but there was no recovery from that train wreck. We finished second in the tournament—unacceptable by Houston standards. With that, my shot at the NCAA team was gone. In the end, John Mahaffey bounced back and qualified for the US Open, and Coach took him to the NCAA Championships at the last minute. And it was the right call. John won the NCAA individual championship, and the University of Houston took the team title for the fourth year in a row.

My shot would have to wait, but that finish in Tucson would stay with me: a very big disappointment and a reminder that I just could not let rounds get away. More grind and more grit was required, and I still had a lot of work to do.

Bill Rogers's "66"

I think it's safe to say that just about everyone who played for Coach Dave Williams at the University of Houston had at least one experience that shocked them so deeply, it stuck with them for life. For Bill Rogers, that moment came early—and he never forgot it.

Bill arrived at Houston in 1970 with a phenomenal junior résumé and sky-high hopes. Coach even offered him a rare multiyear scholarship—a real show of faith in his potential.

THE COACH

Expectations were high but, like most freshmen, Bill struggled. He was thin, didn't hit the ball particularly far, and, to be blunt, was just another guy on a team packed with standout players. Meanwhile, his good friend Bruce "Leaky" Lietzke was making waves, already finding his way onto the team as a freshman. It didn't take long for Bill to feel overshadowed.

Coach had a habit of fielding two teams in smaller tournaments around Houston, where "Team B" often finished just behind "Team A"—a testament to the depth of talent at Houston. Most of the guys on that second team could have been the stars of other programs, and, in some cases, they might have been the best players at those schools. But in Houston, they were just trying to crack the lineup.

Finally, Bill Rogers—who, by this time, had earned the inevitable nickname "Buck"—got a shot at playing on Team B for a tournament held just outside Houston at Pine Forest, which was a tough course. It was a frigid winter day, not exactly ideal golf weather, and the scores were generally higher than usual. But, somehow, Buck found his rhythm. He shot an incredible 66, leading the field by several shots with thirty-six holes still to play the next day.

Naturally, Buck was thrilled. He practically sprinted over to hand Coach his scorecard, no doubt expecting some recognition. Coach took one look at that 66, and you could almost see the gears turning in his mind. In Coach's eyes, Buck was nowhere near the top of Houston's depth chart, but he was clearly on fire. And that presented a problem: There was a chance Buck could go out there, hold his lead, and actually win the tournament. That, apparently, was more than Coach could handle.

So Coach looked up, handed back Buck's scorecard, and told him he didn't need to show up the next day. He was to go back to school. Just like that, the curtain fell.

For Buck, it was a gut punch. He was in shock—one of the best rounds of his life, and instead of praise or encouragement, he got a pat on the back and a "see you on campus." That was it. No more chances to play, at least not for another year. Coach wasn't one to explain his decisions, and Buck was left to make sense of it on his own.

Of course, Buck went on to become a sensational player for Houston. He would become the number one player in all of college golf, then, eventually, the number one player in the world. He won the British Open, racked up wins around the globe, and reached the pinnacle of the sport. But even today, Buck still talks about that day at Pine Forest. It's something he never forgot—one of those moments that defined the journey of a world-class player who, for a time, was just another guy fighting for a spot on a stacked University of Houston golf team.

Losing

To say Coach Williams didn't take losing easily would be the biggest understatement of the century. Losing to the University of Texas? Well, that was like pouring gasoline on a bonfire. And you've got to understand, this wasn't just any Texas team. In 1971 and 1972, they had Ben Crenshaw and Tom Kite—absolute legends in the making—and three more guys who were very solid players with no choke in their games. That team was loaded and would go on to win the NCAA Championship.

THE COACH

We'd just lost the Border Olympics down in Laredo, Texas, which was a tournament Houston had won for decades until Ben and Tom committed to UT. The mood with Coach, after the scores were counted up and UT edged us out, was about as dark as the evening sky. Somehow, as we packed up, a few of us made the mistake of mentioning Ben's last round.

"Crenshaw shot another 63."

"Can you believe he can shoot this low again?"

And just like that, Coach's ears pricked up. He didn't need to hear much more. The fact that we were talking in glowing terms about Ben and giving him rave reviews was enough to set Coach's blood boiling.

Here's where it gets interesting. Bill Rogers happened to be in the front seat with Coach, with two guys in the back seat, for the ride back to Houston. I was in the second car, in Bruce Lietzke's orange Dodge Charger. As the story goes, Coach pulled out of Laredo, his knuckles white on the steering wheel, and started heading down the freeway. But then, not far down the road, Coach pulled the car over and turned to Bill, looking deadly serious, and said, "Buck, open that glove compartment and hand me my pistol."

Bill stared back at him. "Coach . . . what are you going to do?"

Coach, with a straight face and without a hint of humor, said, "I'm gonna kill myself, Buck."

Of course, Bill wasn't about to hand his coach a weapon, no matter how low our second-place finish had made him feel. He tried to reason with him, saying things like, "Coach, we lost a golf tournament, that's all." But Coach was in his own world, staring out at the highway like a man ready to meet his maker.

To this day, Bill says he has no idea what Coach would have done if he'd actually gotten his hands on the gun that may or may not have been in that glove compartment. Bill never opened it to check. Maybe he would've just tossed it out the window in frustration, or maybe he would've taken a couple potshots at a road sign. But that was the kind of intensity Coach had. Winning wasn't just a goal but the only acceptable outcome. Anything short of that, Coach would feel like his world was collapsing.

Bill finally convinced Coach to keep driving, though it wasn't easy. They rode the rest of the way in silence. To this day, he's never forgotten that drive, and neither have we. That story made the rounds fast. It was a little terrifying, but it showed us all just how much Coach cared—and how little room there was for losing.

3

THE LEGENDS

Kicked Off for Good

Jim Simons was already well-known, when he arrived at Houston, as one of the top junior golfers in the country and probably the only freshman in America who'd qualified for not one but *two* US Opens while still in high school. Who wouldn't be impressed? And as if that weren't enough, he'd won the Pennsylvania Junior three years in a row, collecting trophies in the Northeast like they were spare change. So when I found out he'd be my suitemate, I was thrilled to have the opportunity to play with him. Jim bunked with Mike Killian in the room across our shared bathroom, while I roomed with Bruce Ashworth, hoping a bit of Jim's skill might rub off on me through sheer proximity.

Jim and I right away were inseparable during our freshman year, even managing to date twins together at one point. Jim had already played with top tour players and picked up a few tricks, several of which he shared with me. One involved hitting a good shot despite a bush or tree branch interfering with your backswing. Jim would just swing slowly through the branches, then rip his arms and club down and through the shot. I never forgot it and, several times in my life, it worked great and definitely surprised my playing partners. So instead of just chipping out in a tournament, I'd occasionally launch a ball back down the fairway when in a bush or under a low-hanging tree. I learned I could take any sort of backswing and reroute it on the downswing—a revelation back then.

But Jim didn't play his best golf as a freshman, just like I didn't. And that's, of course, a big part of my story here.

Toward the end of the year, we had a mandatory team meeting where Coach outlined the season's wrap-up details and plans for the upcoming NCAA Championship. He also announced that, come Sunday, we'd be playing a round with members at one of the local clubs. The coach arranged these events to secure us playing privileges.

At this point, Jim raised his hand and said, "Coach, I'm not gonna be able to play this Sunday."

Coach replied, "Of course, you're going to play."

Jim explained, "I have to play a practice round for the US Open qualifier, which is on Monday. Sunday's the day for practice rounds."

For a moment time froze in that room. Coach just finally snapped. "You can get your ass back to Butler, Pennsylvania, where you came from! We don't need any more seventy-five shooters on this team!"

And that was that. Jim didn't play in the team event, but he did play in the US Open qualifier, though he barely missed qualifying. Unfortunately, his time with our team was over, and soon enough, he was packing up for Butler.

Jim went on to transfer to Wake Forest University and joined an excellent team, playing with Hall of Famer Lanny Wadkins. Two years later, as a junior, he qualified for the US Open again. This time, he played one of the most remarkable tournaments any amateur has ever played in a professional event. He was the solo leader after three rounds, was paired with Jack Nicklaus in the final round, and just behind him were Billy Casper and Lee Trevino. Talk about a pressure cooker. Jim stayed composed, and going into the last hole, he still had a shot to win before making a double bogey, finishing fifth. It was one of the greatest finishes by an amateur in US Open history.

By the time I was a senior, I felt comfortable enough around Coach to land a well-timed jab. I'd say, "Coach, what a great move getting rid of that seventy-five-shooting Jim Simons!" Coach would just pretend not to hear me and keep moving along.

Later, Jim went on to win four times on the PGA Tour, and we remained friends for many years. I would often drive down to the Doral Resort in Miami with Jim when he worked with top teacher Jimmy Ballard.

RB Qualified

Note: *I'm writing this story from notes my great friend Rick Belden sent to me. I'm writing as if this story were actually written by him, with a little Texas humor and exaggeration by me sprinkled in for good measure.*

I finally *qualified* for the University of Houston golf team in 1971—well, barely. But hey, let's not get picky. Qualified is qualified. For the first time, I was playing in a tournament, and not just any tournament. This was against the University of Texas at Atascocita Golf Course. And let me tell you, there's nothing casual about a UH vs. UT matchup.

We hated UT. I don't mean the kind of hate where you grumble under your breath. I mean the kind that's baked into your soul like a good pecan pie. It wasn't just golf—it was pride, state bragging rights, and proving who really owned Texas. The Longhorns might've had their burnt orange gear and their Austin attitude, but we were the Cougars—determined and ready to take them down.

That said, we couldn't help but be a little impressed by their lineup. Tom Kite and Ben Crenshaw weren't just good—they were *ridiculous*. Future legends, plain and simple. Everyone knew it.

Tom Kite was all business. The guy had a focus so sharp, it could've cut through Texas beef brisket. He had this knack for making you feel like the tournament was over before it even started. And Ben? Well, Ben Crenshaw wasn't just a golfer but rather poetry in motion, especially on the greens. That putting stroke? It looked like it had been handcrafted by angels. You couldn't watch him without shaking your head and muttering, "Damn, that's good."

But boy, could those two whine.

Tom Kite had this thing about his putting. Every time he missed, even from thirty feet out, he'd act like the laws of physics had betrayed him. I remember Jim McLean, leaning over and muttering, "If Kite moans one more time about missing a thirty-footer, I'm gonna deck him." And you know what? I think he meant it.

And then there was Ben. Sweet Ben, with his syrupy Texas drawl and that butter-smooth stroke. But don't let that charm fool you. Every time a putt didn't drop, he'd throw his hands in the air and groan, "How did that ball *not* go in the hole?" Like the ball owed him rent money and refused to pay up.

Meanwhile, I was pleased to be there. I finally had a UH golf bag with my name on it and a shirt that read, "University of Houston." That might not sound like much, but when you're one of thirty-plus guys on the team and most of them *don't* have that bag or shirt? It's a big deal. That bag meant something. It said, "You made it. You're here. You're playing for Houston."

As for the tournament itself, every shot was a battle. Every putt was intense. Every shot was like my life depended on it. I felt like Coach was somewhere out in the woods, lurking and wondering how I was going to hold up. Pressure, yes. I felt the pressure.

In the end, watching Tom and Ben shoot great scores on the same course I was playing was cool. Plus, knowing how our players stacked up that week was a great memory. It was like watching the future of the game unfold right in front of you.

Looking back, that tournament wasn't just a chance to compete. It was also a life lesson. I was part of a great team playing against Tom and Ben and their very talented team. And for one week, I got to compete for Houston, rocking that UH bag and soaking it all in.

That bag was more than a piece of equipment. It was a badge of honor, and it said I was part of something bigger, something legendary. And even though Jim didn't follow through on decking Tom (probably for the best), I'll never forget the sound of Ben groaning, "How did that ball *not* go in the hole?" Some things just stick with you.

Picking up Hogan's Clubs

There are moments in life when opportunity knocks so quietly, you almost miss it, and then there are moments when it kicks the door wide open and dares you to do something. This is the story of one such moment.

I had just spent the day watching Ben Hogan play at Champions Golf Club—certainly one of the great things about playing for the University of Houston. If you've ever seen Ben in action, you know the man was a living legend. He didn't just hit golf balls; he made them sing. Inspired, I hit the range to work on my own game.

As the sun set and the range emptied out, I wandered back into the bag room on my way to the golf shop. My head was still filled with visions of Ben's perfect swing and amazing ball-striking. That's when I saw them.

In the corner of the bag room, sitting there as if they owned the place—because, in a way, they did—were Ben Hogan's golf clubs.

I froze. Was I really staring at *the* clubs of the greatest ball-striker of all time? And more importantly: Was anyone around?

I glanced left. Nobody. I glanced right. Still nobody. It was like the universe had aligned for this moment.

But then the voice of reason: *I better not.*

THE LEGENDS

Don't do it, Jim. Don't even think about it. What if Hogan walks in? What if Jackie Burke or Jimmy Demaret catch you? What would you possibly say? "Oh, I was just, uh, appreciating the craftsmanship"? Yeah, right. You would never live it down. Maybe you would never be allowed back to Champions. And if it was Ben walking in himself—oh my!

But then another voice kicked in—only louder.

Come on. How many people on this planet can say they've held Ben Hogan's clubs? You're already here. Don't blow this opportunity.

And so, I took a step forward. Then another. Before I knew it, I was standing over Ben's bag, like I was about to defuse a bomb.

I reached out and grabbed one of his irons. My hands felt the weight, the balance, the craftsmanship. I examined the oversized grips—the famous ones with the massive reminders that forced your hands into a weak position. They were like commandments etched in rubber.

Then there was his driver. The driver had almost no loft, just as we had all been told. It felt like holding Excalibur, and I half expected it to start glowing in my hands.

For a moment, I imagined Ben walking in. My mind raced with potential scenarios.

Option 1: Drop the club and run. (Not exactly dignified, but effective.)

Option 2: Pretend I'd just tripped and "accidentally" grabbed his clubs to steady myself.

Option 3: Own it. "Oh, Mr. Hogan! Just, uh, inspecting your gear. Top-notch stuff!"

Thankfully, none of that happened. The room stayed silent, and I took it as my cue to carefully, reverently return each club to its rightful place. I cautiously replaced the head cover on the driver and set the bag exactly as I'd found it.

I walked out of that room feeling like I'd just committed a robbery—but also like I'd just been handed the keys to golf's inner sanctum. How many people in history had actually held Ben Hogan's clubs? Not many, I can assure you.

Looking back, I'm glad I took the chance. It was a brief, almost sacred moment for a young golfer trying to understand the essence of greatness. Those clubs were more than tools but rather extensions of Ben himself—symbols of precision, discipline, and mastery.

And while I may not have walked away a better golfer that night, I did walk away with a story. A story about the time I held Ben Hogan's clubs, felt their weight, and somehow managed not to get caught.

Tom Kite: Houston Killer

I've known Tom Kite since our junior golf days, and, let me tell you, that boy has been good for as long as anyone can remember. Small in stature, he had a short game that could challenge the best pros in the sport. As a junior, it didn't seem that Tom was destined to be a World Golf Hall of Fame player. He just didn't have the length, and definitely not the look. But by the time he played at UT, he had changed everyone's mind. Tom Kite would more than live up to the college billing.

Tom had earned himself a scholarship to the University of Texas after his stellar junior career. And he joined what would go down as the most lethal one-two punch in college golf history

THE LEGENDS

when Ben Crenshaw enrolled the next year. If you were playing against the Longhorns, you had to hope everyone on your team played their best because Tom Kite and Ben Crenshaw were going to shoot low numbers. Every week.

In college, I was paired with Tom plenty of times, and playing against Tom Kite was like trying to lasso the wind. Back then, his ball flight was a classic West Texas hook. It was more than a draw. In fact, it was sometimes a rope hook. Just enough for that old balata ball to fly low and run out. A shot I had never seen growing up in the Pacific Northwest.

But just when you thought, *Oh, Tom's in trouble*, his ball would turn left, hit the ground, and start running like a scalded armadillo. By the time it stopped, it had rolled farther than it flew.

He didn't *carry* his driver far at all, but then it would just roll forever. Into a Texas wind, he was money. And if you know anything about Texas, you know the wind there isn't just a breeze; it's a full-on atmospheric assault. But, to Tom, it was like the wind didn't exist. Most of us would be fighting to keep our drives in the ballpark. When I played with Tom in those conditions, his ball would be out there rolling past mine, like it had a motor attached. Of course, I was sometimes hitting up-shoots into that Texas wind. If you hit an up-shoot driver off the bottom of a wooden club, it might cause a balata ball to spin at ten thousand revolutions per minute (or rpms), like a modern-day L-wedge. It backed up even on the concrete-hard Texas fairways. Not good.

I would watch in disbelief, scratching my head like I'd just seen a UFO. "This can't last," I would say. "No way this sorcery holds up."

But round after round, year after year, there he was—cranking out those roller-coaster draws and picking up wins.

The amazing thing was both Ben and Tom were taught by the legendary Texas genius Harvey Penick. Harvey would never let either one of them watch the other get lessons.

You could not imagine such different swings or golf games. And talk about contrasts. While Ben Crenshaw was the golf world's version of a golden-haired rock star, floating around the course with effortless grace, Tom was a scientist—deadly serious, analytical, and built like he just finished a double-meat cheeseburger. His massive knee slide looked like he was trying to dodge an invisible rattlesnake, and his upper body leaned so far back, his spine looked like it could snap at any moment (his spine tilt at impact was about seventy degrees). He had glasses so big and covered his entire head, they could've been issued by NASA. We called them Coke-bottle glasses.

His demeanor on the course? Let's just say Tom wasn't there to chitchat. Smiles were rare, almost nonexistent.

Tom grew up on a putting green. By that, I mean his father, Mr. Tom Kite, built a green in the backyard when young Tom was two. Mr. Kite loved putting. He drove his Saturday afternoon playing companions crazy by making putts from everywhere, every week. So he started Tom early. And, like his father, Tom developed that same love for putting. It's debatable who had the Guinness World Record for consecutive five-footers, but it was either Mr. Kite or Tom.

It was nothing for Tom to putt four hours a day—he loved putting practice like Jimi Hendrix loved practicing his guitar. In other words, nonstop. I have to say, I never knew anyone who "loved putting practice." After thirty minutes or so, putting practice got monotonous. But "monotonous" was Tom's middle name.

In tournaments, Tom poured in eight-footers like they were nothing. At Houston, we often talked about the odds of anyone consistently making every putt under ten feet, but Tom defied the odds. Was it possible that he literally didn't miss, ever, in college? At least it seemed that way against the Houston Cougars. I would come in after completing my round with Tom and tell my teammates, "Surprise, Kite made everything again, turned a 78 into a 66!"

Tom was so methodical, he'd line up *six-inch putts*. I mean, who does that? Most of us would tap those blindfolded while whistling "The Eyes of Texas." But Tom? He acted like every putt had a million dollars riding on it. And maybe that's why he *never* wasted a shot. Not in practice, not in competition, not even in casual rounds. Rumor has it that the last time Tom wasted a shot was when he was six years old, and even then, nobody was quite sure about that.

The guy engineered his game like he was building a spaceship. Every shot had a purpose. Every putt had a plan. Did I mention hitting practice balls? Ben Hogan, Vijay Singh, Tom Kite. The big three of all-time ball-beaters.

Tom Kite wasn't flashy. He wasn't effortless like Ben Crenshaw, who could charm the birds out of the trees with his sweet smile and his Las Vegas gambler's nerves. Ben would love to lay down four aces after you were about to pull in the chips with your full house. Tom, on the other hand, would prefer to buy the SPY in the stock market and let it ride smartly for the rest of his life. What Tom lacked in flair and style, he made up for in pure, unrelenting determination. Playing against him was like trying to out-argue a lawyer who'd memorized the rule book—exhausting, frustrating, and, ultimately, a lost cause.

And that's what made him so incredible. Tom Kite didn't just play golf; he dissected it, calculated it, and tried his best to defeat it. Watching him grind out rounds was a lesson in grit, determination, and the art of proving everyone wrong.

After college, Tom would go on to win *thirty-seven* professional tournaments, including *twenty* on the PGA Tour, plus the US Open. He made the US Ryder Cup team eight times, and topped the money list so often, they probably had his checks printed in advance. He would also work on his golf swing with me for all of 1992, when he won his own US Open at Pebble Beach. On the Monday after that win, I had dinner with Tom Kite and Ben Crenshaw. Just the three of us. One of the more special evenings of my life.

Bill Rogers and Me at the US Open: The Famous Phone Call

Qualifying for the 1971 US Open at the legendary Merion Golf Club was a dream come true for me. I shot 135—71 in the front nine and 64 in the back—to win the regional qualifier for that Open. It was already shaping up to be an unforgettable experience, and it only got better when I learned Bill Rogers had also qualified and that we would be rooming together at the players' hotel.

As fate would have it, in the next room were Lanny Wadkins and Jim Simons—two of my very good friends. Jim had been my roommate at Houston before he transferred to Wake Forest and joined forces with Lanny, who was all swagger and confidence, even at twenty years old. He had already finished second in a PGA Tour event and was one of the favorites to contend at Merion. Meanwhile, Jim was playing his *third* US Open.

The drama started early for me. During a practice round, I teamed up with Jim, Lanny, and Bruce Fleisher, the reigning US Amateur Champion. We stepped up to Merion's famously difficult first hole—one that got tighter the farther you went, with a bunker that narrowed the fairway to 12 yards wide at about 270 yards out. At that point, it was guarded like Fort Knox. The tee box was situated extremely close to the clubhouse, providing a gallery even during regular play, let alone a US Open. We were just preparing to tee off when, suddenly, major champions Billy Casper, Gary Player, Al Geiberger, and Gay Brewer walked up directly behind us on the very small back tee box. I could immediately feel the extra tension.

Lanny, as cocky as they come, pulled out his jumbo-sized driver and stuck a tee in the ground. If you've ever seen the first hole at Merion, you know hitting a driver there is like trying to thread a needle with a fire hose. Gay Brewer saw this and immediately heckled Lanny, "What the hell are you doing hitting a driver here? There's no fairway for a driver. You're not going to hit a driver in this tournament."

Lanny, cool as a Texas summer night, said, "I hit the driver on every hole, Brewer." When Lanny said "Brewer," referring to a Masters Champion, the tension level jumped.

Gay Brewer, now sensing an opportunity, said, "I'll bet you one thousand dollars you can't hit the fairway right now."

Bruce Fleisher immediately said, "I'll take half that bet on Lanny's side."

THE HOUSTON DYNASTY

Unfazed, Lanny grinned, stepped up to the ball, and absolutely nuked the most perfect drive I've ever seen—dead center, splitting the narrow fairway. Without even looking at the ball, Lanny turned to Gay and said, "Brewer, don't ever bet against me, bro."

I'll tell you what—trying to hit my own tee shot after that was like trying to follow Eric Clapton at Wembley Stadium in London. My heartbeat jumped to 180.

So not only did we have major champions standing directly behind us, but we also had a huge gallery listening in and watching. I wished I had hit before Lanny, but no such luck. You know, I just had to crack a smile when I thought of the incredible cockiness to defy Gay Brewer and rip that drive. It was something I would never forget.

The night before the first round, Bill and I were doing our best to stay calm. We talked, watched TV, and tried to act like it was just another tournament. Eventually, we turned out the lights, and I was finally starting to drift off when—at 2 *a.m.*—the phone rang.

Bill and I both shot up, startled, wondering who in the world would be calling us at that hour. I picked up, and who was on the other end but Hilmer Starke. Hilmer, with his thick Southern drawl and unique charm, wanted to let us know he'd be watching our scores the next day.

For those who don't know Hilmer, let me paint a picture: He had a swing that could only be described as *one of a kind*. His clubface at the top of the backswing was so closed, it looked like he was trying to hammer a nail. And when things went wrong—well, let's just say Hilmer could hit a hook like you have never witnessed. His tee shots might have invented the "snipe hook" term. If you played with Hilmer, you turned away, because that hook, or that closed clubface, might invade your swing. Plus, the image of a low pull hook was always a possibility. It was better not to watch.

After we hung up, Bill and I lay in bed, staring at the ceiling. The idea of Hilmer calling us at 2 a.m. suddenly seemed like some kind of cosmic omen. For a while, we couldn't stop laughing as we imagined both of us standing on the first tee, cold sweat dripping down our faces, and hitting the mother of all hooks into the first-aid stand.

It was funny—until it wasn't. Once the laughter died down, the thought of hitting a snipe hook on Merion's first hole stayed with us. That narrow fairway felt like it had shrunk another six yards in my mind, and neither of us slept much after.

When the big day finally arrived, I found myself waiting to tee off in the group directly behind none other than Arnold Palmer—"The King"—who was still in his prime. The gallery, as you can imagine, was massive. There must have been fifteen thousand spectators lining the first hole. You could feel the electricity in the air—all eyes were on him. I watched Arnold tee off and walk down the fairway, the huge crowd following, leaving me with my thoughts—and Hilmer's voice echoing in my head.

By the time I stood over my ball, all I could think was, *Don't hit the Hilmer hook. Don't hit the Hilmer hook.* Somehow, I managed to keep it in play and out of the first-aid tent I had eyed up before swinging.

The tournament itself was amazing. Jim Simons played out of his mind, leading the US Open after three rounds and playing the final round alongside Jack Nicklaus. In the group behind him were Billy Casper and Lee Trevino, who would eventually beat Jack in the playoff. (You might remember Lee threw the fake snake at Jack on the first tee of the playoff.) Jim finished fifth, an incredible performance for an amateur, and Lanny wasn't far behind, finishing eighth—a one-two punch from amateurs that hadn't been seen in decades.

As for Bill and me? Well, let's just say we played okay but missed the cut. Hilmer's phone call, the sleepless night, and the Merion pressure might've had something to do with it.

Still, I wouldn't trade the experience for anything. The laughs, the nerves, and the sheer spectacle of it all—it was pure golf, with a little Texas-sized humor thrown in for good measure. And as for Hilmer? Well, every time I think about that call, I still smile—and maybe grip the club just a little tighter. It certainly made for one of the all-time stories when we got back to the University of Houston.

Watching Ben Hogan

If you've never seen Ben Hogan swing a golf club, let me tell you, it was like watching a master painter in his studio.

This was 1969, and the setting was Champions Golf Club in Houston, where Jackie Burke and Ben were playing a round with Jackie's brother, Jimmy Burke, the head professional at Champions. I got wind of this game on a damp winter day and drove out to witness it.

I got there in time to watch them tee off. You'd think watching Ben Hogan would draw a crowd the size of Texas itself, but there were only four or five spectators there. It was one of those cold, gray Houston days that kept most folks indoors. Very few people knew Ben was in for a visit.

We stayed as close as we could without ever getting in Ben's way. That's the unspoken rule: You didn't ever interfere with Ben when he was practicing or playing. Everyone knew his legendary intensity. The man was a fortress of concentration, and even the thought of drawing his attention made me nervous.

Being close enough to hear their conversation was very cool though. Ben didn't waste words, but when he spoke, you hung on every syllable.

This was the fall of '69, just months after Lee Trevino shocked the world by winning the US Open at Oak Hill. Lee had done the impossible: four rounds in the '60s to claim his first major championship.

Yet, despite his performance, there was plenty of skepticism about Lee. Why? Well . . .

- He played with a Band-Aid on his left arm to cover a tattoo of an old girlfriend's name.
- His pants were too short, and he wore red socks that looked more suited for a barn dance than the PGA Tour.
- And his golf swing? It was unconventional, to say the least. Most experts doubted he would last.

Lee's swing was so different from Ben's, it seemed almost impossible to compare the two. Ben's swing was a study in symmetry and precision, while Lee's looked very odd, with a huge head dip. Lee also set the club in a completely different position at the top—flat, closed, and laid-off—compared to Ben's low left arm and open clubface at the top. For many, that was enough to dismiss him as a fluke.

As we quietly followed the group, I heard Jackie Burke ask Ben the question everyone in golf was whispering about.

"Ben," Jackie said, "do you think Trevino's swing will last?"

There wasn't a moment's hesitation. Hogan answered immediately: "Lee Trevino is not going away. I love the way he flights the golf ball, and I love that fade he controls so well."

Lee could see the future. To him, it didn't matter how unconventional Lee's swing looked. What Ben saw was what mattered most: control, ball flight, and consistency.

That simple, direct answer hit me like a lightning bolt. Ben's approval wasn't just validation for Lee's swing—it was a testament to what truly mattered in golf. Ben didn't necessarily care about aesthetics or tradition. He cared about results.

What struck me even more was Ben's admiration for Lee's ability to flight the ball and his mastery of the controlled fade. Coming from Ben, the man who'd spent a lifetime perfecting his ability to shape shots under any conditions, that was the ultimate compliment.

I couldn't stop thinking about that exchange. Ben had spent years building a swing that was considered the gold standard of technique. Lee's swing, by comparison, was unorthodox and borderline homemade. But Ben didn't see it that way.

He didn't mention the flat position at the top or the unpolished appearance. What Ben saw was Lee's repeatability: his ability to hit the same shot over and over, no matter the pressure.

Ben had said it all in just a few words: "Lee Trevino is not going away." And Ben was right. Lee's swing did last, and it did repeat. The quirks didn't matter because, underneath them, there was something Ben revered above all else: consistency and control.

Lee went on to win six majors, dominate in match play, and become one of the most beloved figures in golf history. His swing may have baffled traditionalists, but it worked. And in the end, Ben's prediction about Lee's staying power wasn't just correct—it was prophetic.

I remember the golf that day at Champions. But what stayed with me was Ben's instant and unwavering respect for Lee. In just a few words, Ben reminded me—and everyone else—that greatness in golf isn't about how it looks. It's about what works.

"Lee Trevino is not going away."

No one could argue with that—not then, not now, and not ever.

Trevino and the Fade

Years later, when I was the director of golf at Sleepy Hollow Country Club from 1988 to 1993, I got to know Lee Trevino during a senior tour we hosted. I hung out with him as much as possible: in the locker room, on the range, and on the course. By that time, Lee's reputation as one of the greatest ball-strikers in golf history was firmly established, but I couldn't help revisiting the conversation I overheard years earlier between Ben Hogan and Jackie Burke at Champions Golf Club.

Curious, I brought it up to Lee. I told him about watching Ben at Champions and Jackie's question. I told him Ben's immediate and emphatic response: "Lee Trevino is not going away. I love the way he flights the golf ball and controls that fade."

Lee's face lit up as I mentioned Ben. It was clear how much he respected the man who had set the gold standard for ball-striking. And then Lee shared something that gave me a deeper appreciation for both his journey and his swing.

"When I was coming up in Texas," Lee said, "I went to watch Hogan practice. Everybody wanted to hit the ball like Hogan. Everybody. And believe me, I tried."

Lee explained how he went home after watching Ben and did his best to copy what he had seen. But the results were disastrous.

"All I could hit was a low hook," he said, with a shake of his head. "It drove me crazy. Sure, I could get the ball around the course—good enough to win money matches I played—but that ball flight wasn't acceptable for the PGA Tour. Not if you wanted to take on the best."

That low hook might have worked for a short term, but Lee knew it wouldn't hold up under the pressures of championship golf. He needed a shot shape he could trust.

"So I went to work," he said. "I kept opening up my stance—aiming farther and farther left—and guess what? The more I opened up, the higher and straighter my shots went. Eventually, I found the fade, and once I did, I never let it go. I worked on it relentlessly."

Lee's process was entirely self-taught. He didn't have access to video analysis, high-speed cameras, or biomechanical breakdowns. His overriding philosophy wasn't about what his swing *looked like* but rather what the golf ball was doing.

"People can get too caught up in the beauty of their swings," Lee said. "But the ball doesn't lie. I wasn't trying to make a pretty swing. I was trying to make a swing that worked. And that fade? It worked."

THE LEGENDS

The adjustments Lee made were significant. His swing didn't look like Ben's at all, whose swing was quick but textbook-perfect. Lee's swing, by contrast, was flat, laid off at the top, and uniquely his own. But in one critical way, Lee did emulate Ben: his ball flight.

Both Ben and Lee mastered the controlled fade: the shot that gave them total control over their trajectory and eliminated one side of the golf course. For Lee, this transformation didn't happen overnight. It was the result of years of trial and error, hard work, and his relentless competitive spirit.

When I think about the great ball-strikers I've spoken to—players who truly understand the art of controlling the golf ball—they always mention two names that stand above the rest: Ben Hogan and Lee Trevino.

The reason is simple: Both of them "owned" their swings. They didn't chase trends or try to fit into molds. They built swings that worked under the most extreme pressure, focusing on what the ball was doing instead of how their swing looked. And in doing so, they achieved mastery few have ever reached.

As I listened to Lee recount his journey, I couldn't help but think of how Ben's words from that cold day in Houston had been so prophetic. Ben had seen what so many others had overlooked: Lee wasn't just another quirky player with an unconventional swing. He was a ball-striking genius in the making; someone who understood the game at its core.

And as I stood there at Sleepy Hollow, listening to him recount his journey, I felt lucky to have seen both men's brilliance up close, each of them proving that the ball flight was all that matters.

4

THE CHARACTERS

The Weed

If there was ever a character to walk the hallowed halls of the University of Houston golf program, it was Bobby "The Weed" Walzel. Bobby wasn't just a golfer—he was a full-blown UH legend in the making. The man could charm the socks off a rattlesnake and still find time to drain a twenty-footer for a birdie.

Bobby's family owned a jewelry store, so he always looked sharp. I mean *real sharp*. It was a real Rolex dealer, and Bobby usually had a ten-thousand-dollar gold Rolex on his wrist for good measure.

His clothes all came from Harold's of Houston, one of the top men's clothing stores in the city. Once you made the team, Harold would provide the top UH players with slacks and shirts, and maybe even a sport coat. But you had to make the team to do that, and Bobby wasn't quite there yet.

Most of us were scraping by like regular college kids, but not Bobby. He had a closet full of pressed slacks, crisp shirts, and cowboy boots that looked like they'd been spit-shined. And then there was the watch—one from the family store that screamed, "I don't just know what time it is, I *own* time."

But what really set Bobby apart was his money clip. Oh, the money clip. Every college kid I knew carried maybe five dollars in crumpled ones if they were lucky. Bobby? He strutted around with a one-thousand-dollar bill on the *outside* of his clip, flanked by a fan of crisp one-hundred-dollar bills. We learned later it was a fake one-thousand-dollar bill, which was to be expected. Was he a college golfer or a traveling oil baron? He definitely looked the part.

But "The Weed" wasn't just about looks and cash. No, his crowning achievement came during the All-American Tournament. Let me set the scene: This was one of the biggest college golf events of the year, and each team had a chaperone from the University of Houston. And when I say "chaperone," I mean gorgeous Texas girls who could make even the steeliest golfer forget how to hold a club.

Well, Bobby decided he wasn't going to impress these ladies with just his wardrobe or his stack of cash. No, sir. He had to take it up a notch.

So, on the way to the tournament, Bobby pulled into a Chevrolet dealership. Most college kids wouldn't have even bothered setting foot in a place like that unless they were lost. But Bobby strolled in like he was there to buy the whole showroom. He gave the dealer his name and mentioned the family business—Walzel Jewelers—and suddenly the guy was treating Bobby seriously.

"I'd like to take a Corvette out for a demo drive," Bobby said, as cool as a spring breeze.

Now, let me tell you, the idea of a *college kid* getting handed the keys to a brand-new Corvette is about as likely as a hole-in-one on a par five. But, somehow, "The Weed" makes it happen. Maybe it was the one-thousand-dollar bill, or maybe it was just pure Texan confidence. Either way, the dealer handed him the keys, and Bobby promised he'd "just drive it around the block."

Yeah, right.

Instead, Bobby floored it and took off to Atascocita, where the tournament was being held. He got the top down, wind in his hair, and a big ol' grin on his face. By the time he arrived, the Corvette was more than a car—it was a party on wheels. Bobby started giving rides to the chaperones, showing off like he was James Bond at a Texas hoedown. And you better believe those girls were impressed.

Meanwhile, the rest of us were standing there with our jaws on the ground. A *college kid* just waltzed into a dealership, grabbed a Corvette, and turned it into his personal limo service.

Eventually, Bobby rolled back into the dealership, cool as could be, like nothing happened. He tossed the keys back to the dealer and probably said something like, "Drives like a dream. Thanks, partner."

How he didn't end up in jail is beyond me. Maybe his dad had some friends at the police department, or maybe the dealership didn't want to admit they'd just handed a ten-thousand-dollar car—which was a fortune back then—to a college kid. Whatever the case, Bobby walked away scot-free, as pretty as you please.

When we asked him how he pulled it off, he just shrugged and said, "It wasn't a problem. They were happy I liked the car."

Nobody knew how he possibly got away with this one. But, somehow, "The Weed" did it.

The Beer Bet: When Rice Took Us to School

Let me introduce you to Jim Barker, better known as "Cat-Man." This guy was world-class at everything involving risk, drinking, athleticism, or any combination of the three. If there were a PhD for beer-drinking, Cat-Man would've graduated summa cum laude. He could chug a tall boy faster than a rattlesnake strike, and we were all convinced he held some sort of unofficial world record. On our University of Houston golf team, this wasn't a matter of opinion. It was *fact*. Cat-Man was a legend.

Apparently, his reputation spread like wildfire across Houston. It got so big that a group of guys from Rice University, Texas's crown jewel of academia, decided to challenge him. And let me tell you, when Rice University showed up, it was like MIT rolling into town, but with Texas swagger. Rice wasn't just smart—it was *scary smart*. People at Rice built robots for fun, calculated pi for breakfast, and probably designed NASA rockets as a senior project. Meanwhile, over at UH, if you knew how to find the library, you were likely a standout student.

Don't get me wrong, UH had plenty of grit and talent, and smart folks too. But Rice was several steps up. When it came to beer-drinking contests though? We were confident. Rice might've had geniuses, but genius doesn't chug beer—it over-analyzes it. So, naturally, when they challenged the Cat-Man, we didn't even hesitate.

THE CHARACTERS

The Rice guys pulled into the UH parking lot, and we were licking our chops. This was a sure thing. Easy money. We all started waving ten-dollar bills like we were at a rodeo auction. Even when their guy climbed out of the van looking like Paul Bunyan, we didn't flinch. Sure, he was about three hundred pounds of pure beer-drinking potential, but we had the Cat-Man. Size didn't matter—speed did.

Then came the bad sign. Rice Dude brought his *own* special tall boy beer can. That alone was very sketchy, but when he revealed a hole at the side of the can, our jaws hit the floor.

"I'll drink from the side," he announced. Was this beer physics? He wasn't going to drink this beer—he was going to *inhale* it.

Were we stupid? Well, not completely—we immediately cried foul. Rules are rules, and holes in cans were *not* in the rule book. The Rice crew looked disappointed but shrugged and started heading back to their van.

That should've been the end of it. But then one of us—probably someone who had just taken a freshman-level physics course—said, "Wait a minute. Let's think this through." After all, Cat-Man could slam a tall boy in under two seconds (practically supernatural). Could this Rice guy really beat that?

So, against all logic, we shouted, "Bet's back on!" Big mistake.

The contest started and, before we could even blink, the Rice guy popped his can, turned it sideways, and *shotgunned* that beer in one second flat. One second. It wasn't drinking; it was high-speed beer extraction. Cat-Man put up a valiant effort, but even his legendary chugging skills couldn't keep up. Rice Dude edged him out, and just like that, the smartest school in Texas walked off with all our money.

We were stunned. Not just broke but humiliated. Rice had outthought, outdrank, and outplayed us. We realized too late that we'd been outclassed not just in beer physics but in common sense. That day, Rice was more than a top academic institution. It was also the undisputed champion of drinking strategy.

More Crazy Bets with the Cat-Man

There wasn't a single wild stunt Jim Barker wouldn't attempt. Nothing. Nada. Zip. They didn't call him "Cat-Man" for nothing. This man had more lives than a barnyard outdoor cat, and a flair for betting that bordered on lunacy. If there was even a whiff of danger, Jim would sniff it out like a hound on the trail and then wager his reputation—and most likely his life—on it.

Let me tell you about just a *few* of the bets that cemented his status as the one and only Cat-Man.

The Ketchup Incident
One day, after an especially boring lunch in Baldwin House, Cat-Man decided he needed to spice things up—literally. He slapped a bottle of ketchup on the table and declared, "Bet y'all a twenty I can drink this whole thing straight." Most people would've taken that as a joke and moved on. But not Cat-Man. When we didn't believe him, he unscrewed the cap and tipped that bottle back like it was a cold Lone Star Beer on a hot Texas day.

THE CHARACTERS

We watched in awe as the thick, red sludge disappeared faster than a rattlesnake into a prairie hole. By the time he slammed the empty bottle down, half the room was dry heaving, and the other half was handing over their cash. He wiped his mouth like a gunslinger cleaning his pistol and said, "Tastes better than slow-cooked barbecue."

The Dryer
Then there was the time he looked at a dorm-room dryer and announced, "Bet I can fit in there, and y'all can turn it on. I'll take all bets I can't do it." If you've ever seen a dorm-room dryer, you know it's larger than normal—but hardly built to hold a full-grown man. But Cat-Man shimmied in like a contortionist at a county fair.

With a little help from some of the players, we shoved him in like we were stuffing a turkey. He fit. "Fire it up!" he hollered from inside, and we did. The dryer started spinning, and so did Cat-Man. They expected him to come out like a broken piñata, but no. When they opened the door, he popped out, grinning like a possum in a cornfield. "Easiest fifty bucks I ever made," he said, staggering a little.

The Swamp Bet
Let's get to the crown jewel of Cat-Man's bets: the one that made us all question not just his sanity but our own for encouraging him. One day, he casually mentioned he could make it across the swamp at Texaco Golf Club. This wasn't just any swamp. This was the kind of swamp that made grown men shudder. It was

full of water moccasins, snapping turtles, and probably a gator or two lying in wait like something out of a horror movie. The water was dark as midnight and thicker than the sludge from an East Texas oil well. Oh, and let's not forget the trees growing straight out of it, which only added to the eerie "don't mess with this" vibe.

Cat-Man just smiled. "Bet I can swim across," he said, as if it were no bigger deal than wading through a kiddie pool. To make it even crazier, he declared he'd do it at *night*.

So about fifteen of us piled into cars and drove out to the swamp one muggy Texas evening. The moonlight barely lit the path as we trudged from the parking lot out to the golf course, the air thick with the sound of crickets and the occasional splash of something *large* moving in the water. By the time we got to the edge of the swamp, most of us were sweating bullets—and not just from the heat.

The bets were laid down, and Cat-Man stood at the edge of the water, ready to dive in like some kind of backwoods Olympian. He had this look in his eye that said, "I've got this." And you know what? He probably did. But as we all stood there, watching him about to risk life and limb for a hundred bucks, something clicked.

"Wait a minute," someone said. "You can't do this, Cat-Man. We can't let you. You're gonna get eaten alive out there!"

The rest of us chimed in, nodding. None of us wanted to explain to Coach why one of his golfers had gone missing in a snake-and-gator-infested swamp. As much as we loved a good bet, this one felt like the line we just couldn't cross.

Cat-Man looked disappointed—almost insulted—but he took it in stride. "Fine," he said. "Y'all are just scared I'd make it, and you'd lose your money." We handed over the cash, anyway, deciding it was better to pay up than watch ol' Cat-Man become a midnight snack.

To this day, we all wonder if he really could've made it across that swamp. Knowing Cat-Man, he probably would've swum halfway, wrestled a gator just for kicks, and come out on the other side grinning like he'd just won the Texas State Lottery. But some mysteries are better left unsolved.

Jim Barker wasn't just fearless—he was downright Texas reckless. But, somehow, he always came out on top, a little richer and a lot more legendary. To this day, whenever I see a bottle of ketchup, a dorm-room dryer, or a swamp, I think of Cat-Man and his wild bets. They don't make 'em like that anymore.

And thank God for that—one Cat-Man was more than enough for a lifetime. Oh, and did I mention he had a great golf game? You would think he took chances out on the course, and, yes, of course, if there was a 5 percent chance he could carry a tree on a dogleg, he was all in. Lakes held no fear. He'd aim at the edge. While golf doesn't lend itself to crazy risk-taking, it did lead to Cat-Man getting through tour school and playing briefly on the PGA Tour. Not many can say that!

Arthur vs. The Texas Pin: A Tale of Golf and Wind

It was a cold winter day at Forest Cove Golf Course, just outside Houston. If you've never experienced Texas cold, let me explain: It's not that "dry chill" folks up north brag about. No, this was forty degrees of bone-chilling, damp air, coupled with a thirty-mile-per-hour north wind that could make a cowboy reconsider his career choices. But we were playing a tournament, and there was virtually no weather that could stop us from playing in Texas.

This story is about one of our top players, Arthur Russell, playing the second hole at Forest Cove. Arthur always seemed to get the short end of the stick, even though he was a fabulous ball-striker and considered by many to be the best junior golfer in America before his arrival to UH. The second hole was the stuff of nightmares: uphill, 230 yards, over a lake, and with a green so narrow, you'd think it was designed by someone who hadn't seen the back tees. And, of course, Coach had us teeing off from the very back, because nothing said "manning up" like a near-impossible shot in miserable weather.

Enter Arthur Russell, one of the best long iron players on the planet. Arthur wasn't just good with a 1-iron—he made that club sing. With the flagstick located at the front part of the green, the rest of us were hitting a 3-wood shot, making sure to clear the lake, while Arthur decided to take on this beast of a hole with the 1-iron.

And, oh, what a shot it was. Pure. As dead-center contact as anyone could ever imagine. If you've ever hit the sweet spot on a cold day, you know that feeling: It's like butter. The wind didn't even matter. That ball was a laser beam, headed straight for the pin.

But here's the thing about golf: It sometimes has a cruel sense of humor. Arthur's perfect shot didn't just *hit* the pin. It collided with it like a freight train. And this wasn't your ordinary flagstick but rather one of those thick, wind-resistant Texas pins, built to survive hurricanes and the occasional tornado. The sound of the impact was like a rifle shot echoing through the course.

THE CHARACTERS

What happened next defied logic and physics: The ball ricocheted off the pin, flying thirty yards *straight back* into the lake. Thirty yards! It didn't trickle off into the water or roll off the green. It took flight backward like it had been launched from a cannon.

Arthur stood there, stunned, as if the golf gods themselves had decided to smite him. The rest of us? Only two players on our team actually saw the shot, but we all definitely heard every detail once we finished the round.

Arthur had to drop behind the lake and try again, but the golf gods weren't done with him. His third shot, after dropping with the penalty stroke, was frazzled by nerves and the howling wind. It didn't make it to the green. Instead, it spun back down the hill into a lie so bad, it looked like the ball had been buried by an angry armadillo.

He hacked out of that junk but came up short again, then he thinned his next pitch shot across the green, where it stopped on the fringe. Now lying 5, Arthur faced a putt that was downhill, downgrain, and downwind, essentially putting on ice with a leaf blower at his back. His first putt barely made it halfway. His second rolled eight feet past. His third? Mercifully in the hole for a snowman, or, in golf terms, an 8.

Arthur shuffled to the third tee box, looking like a man who'd just lost his ranch in a poker game. And who could blame him? It was forty degrees, the wind was howling, and he had sixteen more holes to go. Somehow, he managed to limp his way to a gritty 81—an admirable score for most mortals in those conditions. But not for Coach. Oh, no. When Arthur turned in his card, Coach didn't even look up. He just shook his head and muttered, "Pathetic." Coach didn't tolerate scores in the 80s, no matter the weather, the course, or the circumstances. To him, Arthur's story was just another excuse, and excuses didn't fly in Houston golf.

Arthur's tragic 8 on that par-3 after a perfectly struck 1-iron was a master class in how quickly this game can humble you. One moment, you're hitting the perfect shot, dead center on the sweet spot. The next, you're staring at a penalty stroke, a buried lie, and an unplayable putt.

Golf, like life, doesn't always reward perfection. Sometimes, it takes your best effort and flings it thirty yards into the nearest lake. But here's the thing: You've got to keep swinging. Arthur finished that round, and it was a testament to his grit.

Years later, we still tell this story—not just because it's hilarious in hindsight, but because it's a reminder of how unpredictable this game can be. And, yes, we laughed. Hard. Because, as horrifying as it was to witness, it's always a little easier when it's not you.

So the next time your perfect shot takes a detour into disaster, just think of Arthur and his 1-iron. And remember: Golf doesn't owe you a thing.

Arturo Russell, Fear Not

Arthur Russell was a guy who, if he feared anything in life, sure didn't show it in a car. When he got behind the wheel of his GTX, he had a point to prove—to the road, to his passengers, and to Bill Rogers, who was best friends with Bruce Lietzke. Bruce was a car aficionado, and Arthur knew it.

THE CHARACTERS

I guess Arthur had something to prove to Bill. He knew Bruce was a fast driver, but Arthur was better. The rest of us had enough sense to steer clear of ever riding with him, but every so often, someone got caught in his whirlwind. Bill Rogers found himself in just that spot one day, and came out of it with a tale that became the stuff of Cougar legend.

The story goes that, for some inexplicable reason, Bill had no choice but to accept a ride with Arthur out to a qualifier in Atascocita. Knowing that Bill was tight with Bruce, Arturo Russell, as we sometimes called him, was dead set on making an impression. Bruce, after all, wasn't just a golf buddy—he was a bona fide car fanatic with his own souped-up Dodge Charger, known to put the pedal to the metal himself. And Arthur wasn't about to miss the opportunity to show Bill that he, too, could live life in the fast lane.

They pulled out of the University of Houston and, before Bill knew it, they were speeding down I-45, heading toward the golf course. Soon enough, they hit FM 1960—a stretch of road so straight and flat, it could've doubled as a landing strip. Lined with telephone poles that seemed to stretch on forever, it was the perfect track for anyone with a lead foot—and Arturo's foot was as heavy as they come.

With a quick glance over at Bill, who was starting to look a little green, Arturo decided it was time to unleash the beast. He floored the gas pedal, and that GTX—a monster with a 460-cubic-inch Hemi engine—let out a roar that practically shook the surrounding trees. The car launched forward with the kind of force that left Bill plastered against his seat, wide-eyed and white-knuckled, bracing for dear life.

Bill would later swear he tried to speak, tried to say something reasonable like, "Hey, maybe we don't need to break the sound barrier on the way to a golf tournament," but it was like his voice had been sucked right out of him. No words would come out. The car was tearing down the road so fast, the telephone poles lining FM 1960 started blending together into a single, unbroken blur—a wall of wood and wire zipping past at what felt like light speed.

And then there was Arturo, calm as ever, with just one finger on the wheel, right foot welded to the floor, grinning like a maniacal cartoon character. Meanwhile, Bill was convinced he was staring down his own obituary. The speed, the roar, the blur—it was a surreal, high-stakes thrill ride, and he was trapped in it.

Somehow, miraculously, they made it to Atascocita in one piece. As soon as Arturo parked, Bill stumbled out of that GTX, dropped to his hands and knees, and kissed the ground like he'd just stepped off a roller coaster from hell. He was as pale as a ghost and too shaken to look Arturo in the eye. But Arturo just grinned, as if he hadn't nearly sent his passenger into the next life.

From that day on, Bill's story became a legendary warning for all Houston Cougars: If you valued your life, you'd think twice before hitching a ride with Arthur Russell.

Ashworth Beats Me Again

The first time I met Bruce Ashworth was in the second round of the US Junior in Oklahoma City. I was fresh off a solid win in my first match, starting to get used to the brutal Oklahoma summer heat, and, frankly, feeling pretty good about my chances. I figured this Ashworth guy would be just another competitor to grind through. Little did I know, I was about to begin a four-year saga of misery against one of the finest—and honestly, one of the luckiest—golfers I'd ever encountered.

Through the first five holes, I was up by one and feeling sharp. On the sixth hole, I hit a beautiful approach shot that stopped about ten feet from the pin. I was already visualizing myself sinking the putt and pulling further ahead, thinking about winning the whole tournament. This match was just a stepping stone. Then Bruce stepped up with a 7-iron and, without so much as a blink, holed it from the fairway for a 2. Just like that, we're back to even. I stood there, shaking my head, thinking, *Alright, one lucky shot. I've still got this.*

On the very next hole, Bruce, looking annoyingly calm, lined up a putt that must have been sixty feet long from off the green; a real monster with about four different breaks in it. The kind of putt you might make once in a hundred tries, if you're lucky. But wouldn't you know it, he knocked it right in. The ball curled and slithered its way like it was on rails, and dropped straight into the cup. Now I was one down and beginning to wonder what the heck was happening. Two miracle shots back-to-back, without even being on the green? No one was that lucky.

Next up, the eighth hole, a long par-3. I needed to stop the bleeding. It looked like my luck had finally turned when Bruce hit his approach shot way off to the right, ending up in what I could only describe as a ditch—a dry creek bed about four feet deep. I figured, *Finally, he's out of the hole.* I strolled over to the green, practically whistling, certain that this was the moment the universe would balance itself out.

But then I saw Bruce, cool as a cucumber, climb down into the creek like he was on a rescue mission. I thought, *What's he even doing? Just take the drop, man.* But no, he had other plans. Next thing I knew, I heard this thump and saw his club shaft flash through the air. I could barely see his head. Before I could even fathom what was happening, his ball popped out, high and perfect, soaring right at the pin like it had a homing device. It bounced, rolled, and slammed into the flagstick. Another 2 on the card. I could've sworn I heard the golf gods laughing in the distance. This three-hole stretch of miraculous shots was so crazy, I just couldn't recover. Though I played well on the way in, I lost 2–1.

But that day was just the beginning. When I chose the University of Houston, Bruce became my roommate. We became fantastic friends and teammates, but that didn't stop him from edging me out in bets and tournaments time and time again. It seemed like "Ashmo" always found some ridiculous way to come out on top in our bets. Sure, I won a few, but Bruce played his best golf every time we played for cash—or he'd pull off some miraculous shot at the end of a bet to win a press.

Did I mention that Bruce wore glasses? Big, thick glasses, which was already a bit annoying. After he would do something to win a bet with me, he would start laughing and bob his head up and down to the center of the glasses. Double-annoying to me!

It became a running theme: If there was a miracle shot to be had against me in a bet, Bruce would pull it off. And, boy, did he love it. He would laugh and remind me for the rest of the evening.

THE CHARACTERS

For a little background, it's worth remembering that Bruce Ashworth was, if not the best college player in the country, then easily one of the top three during this time. He was the number one player on the University of Houston national championship team as a sophomore, a First-Team All-American. So it wasn't just me he routinely took to the woodshed. I had nothing but the utmost respect for his beautiful golf game, consistent ball-striking, and one of the smoothest putting strokes you'd ever seen.

Fast-forward to my junior year, and I was absolutely done losing to this guy. Bruce was a senior, and I was determined to finally beat him in something significant before he graduated.

So my best chance came in the spring of 1971. We were competing in a college tournament in Houston, and, for once, it looked like I was not only going to win but Bruce was going to finish second. Perfect!

It was a two-horse race for the individual win. Houston was going to win the team title easily. When I finished my round (a fifty-four-hole event), I had a solid two-shot lead over Bruce, with nobody else close. Bruce was two back with two holes to go, so I figured he was safely in my rearview mirror.

But, just as I was ready to start celebrating the individual win, someone came over and said, "Hey, you know Ashworth just drained a long birdie putt on seventeen."

I tried to brush it off. *Good for him*, I thought, *but it's not going to be enough.* He still had a difficult eighteenth hole to play, and the odds were good he wouldn't birdie that one too.

Now I'm standing behind the eighteenth green with a few spectators, watching as Bruce hit a long iron to the green. It was an excellent shot, but still about thirty feet away. Could that possibly happen again?

Yes, it could! *Bam!* Slam dunk by Ashmo. I shook my head, thinking, *Unbelievable*. He birdied the last two holes. But I had to admit, when he stood over that putt on the eighteenth, I was expecting him to make it. Karma always had a way of showing up.

Next we're headed to a playoff, and I'm determined not to let this win slip through my fingers—or, rather, be ripped out of my hands by Ashworth yet again.

The pressure was on, but I was beyond ready. I told myself that I wasn't losing to him again. I'd suffered years of too many ridiculous defeats and miracle shots, and I was determined to make this one different. We both headed out for the first playoff hole, and I was locked in, more focused than I'd ever been.

Then, on the first hole, I miraculously sank a forty-foot putt for a birdie, and I was practically floating. I ran up and picked my ball out of the hole. Now I had him for sure. I'd definitely shocked Ashmo with my own unexpected bomb!

Bruce had a twenty-five-footer left, and this one was a beast: With a break so nasty, it might as well have a switchback halfway to the hole. I thought, *There's no way he's making this one*. There was no karma that could take this win from me. I even took my glove off, put my putter back in the bag, and started thinking about how great it'd feel to shake his hand in victory. I was already smiling, awaiting my moment.

But I should have known better. As Bruce rolled his putt, I watched the ball climb the first hill, take the insane break, and start picking up speed. It was going way too fast. *There's no way this is dropping*, I thought, practically daring fate to prove me

THE CHARACTERS

wrong. And then—*wham!*—it went dead center, like a rat diving into its burrow. I just stood there, in disbelief, while he gave me that look, centering his glasses, and cackling like only he could. It was disgusting. His glee made it one hundred times worse.

The wind was knocked out of my sails. I was so rattled I bogeyed the next hole. I couldn't recover. Bruce had done it to me again, pulling out a win from the jaws of defeat, leaving me to wonder if he had some kind of mystical deal with the golf gods.

And that was how it went, time after time. Somehow, he always found a way, and I ended up standing on the sideline, shaking my head. Looking back, maybe it was his calm, his pure talent for the game, or just his uncanny knack for pulling off the seemingly impossible. Whatever it was, Bruce Ashworth had my number. And as much as it drove me crazy, watching him pull off those shots was something I wouldn't trade for anything.

The Root Beer Ball

Corker DeLoach from McMinnville, Tennessee, was one of a kind, but Coach never bothered with all that. To him, Corker was just "McMinnville," pure and simple. That was the only name Coach ever called him, which was pretty much the only simple thing about Corker. The guy could play golf like nobody's business, though he had a swing that made you want to reach for eye drops. Imagine a Sam Snead swing, then strip it of all the grace and add a lashing, thrashing energy—like a whip gone rogue.

Corker, or "CD," as we called him, had his own brand of golf magic. His favorite move? Teeing up his ball on a pencil, taking a stance so wide you'd think he was preparing for a tornado, then swinging with all the fury he could muster. Nine times out of ten, that ball would soar down the fairway, and Corker would holler, "Root beer ball! How was that?" None of us had the slightest clue what root beer had to do with it, but it seemed to work for him, so we didn't ask questions. CD loved nothing more than to belt out "root beer ball!" as he sent his driver screaming down the fairway, usually with a grin that suggested he'd just cracked the code to life.

Being a Tennessee native, CD held true to some time-honored traditions. Chief among them was a deep love for Tennessee whiskey—a drink he'd down like it was a glass of water. And just as naturally, he smoked like a chimney. This was all fine and dandy, except Coach had a strict "no smoking, no drinking" rule for his players. As far as Coach was concerned, his players were supposed to be choirboys—at least when he was watching.

Of course, CD was a master at sneaking around this rule. He'd puff on "ciggys," as he called them (which we all assumed was Tennessee slang, the way he said it). He figured he was in the clear as long as Coach didn't catch him, but inevitably, once in a while, Coach would catch him mid-puff. He would look CD dead in the eye, kick him off the team on the spot, and declare justice served. But with CD, "kicked off" never really lasted long. By the next day—sometimes even sooner—he'd be back on the team like nothing had happened. If lesser players had been caught smoking, they would have been gone for months, but not CD. He was a Houston "stud player." He earned All-American honors for three consecutive years—1970, 1971, and 1972—and was the team MVP in Houston's 1970 NCAA Championship victory, where he tied for seventh individually. He also competed in the 1970 US Open, showcasing his unique talents on a national stage.

CD always had a way of smoothing things over that made even Coach throw his hands up. It didn't really matter what crazy things he might do at school or somewhere else away from school. CD also had a way with words that could calm a storm.

Early on, Coach found out that CD wasn't just dating; he was living with his beautiful girlfriend, Ann. In fact, CD had arrived at the University of Houston already living with her, which didn't sit well with Coach. So, being Coach, he invited the young couple to his house, sat them both down, and said, "Now, listen here, this is just not right. If you're going to live together, you better make it official." And that's exactly what CD did. He married Ann that week, and they stayed happily married for the rest of his life.

Corker DeLoach passed away in 2017, and Ann is still back home in Tennessee, living proof that a little rule-breaking, a lot of charm, and a golf swing you'd never find in a textbook are sometimes all you need.

Brother Brow

Of all the unlikely golfers I've seen, or who have ever arrived at the University of Houston to play on the golf team, the most unlikely had to be Bobby Brown. We immediately named him Brother Brow. Why? It just seemed right.

Brother Brow was about five feet, three inches tall—if he was wearing his high-tops. He wore thick glasses that sat unusually sideways on his face, the jet-black rims highlighting the crooked look. His hair was a bushed mess, wild and unkempt.

Brother Brow usually had a ketchup stain somewhere on his untucked shirt, and his pants were always too long. I guess he overestimated his inseam by several inches.

Yet this guy could really play. He stepped up to the ball looking like a professional, albeit with the clothes still overwhelming your vision. Then he swung—wow! It was majestic, and the ball exploded off the clubface. Who would ever believe it?

Brother Brow had an awesome personality that immediately won him friendships with everyone. You couldn't help but like the guy. His best friend at Houston was six-foot-eight Robert Hoyt, and it wasn't until after I left Houston that these two were paired together in college tournaments. When they walked up together, I could only imagine what the other teams must have thought. Was this some kind of joke? And then Brother Brow and Robert Hoyt would put a Houston Cougar–whipping on the unsuspecting competition. Both would go on to be super successful!

The Cougars In A Romp

• **The** University of Houston's golf team not only keeps winning, it breaks records along the way. Latest came in the 5th annual Bill Shelton Invitational at Houston.

The Cougars scored 1,087 to erase the 1967 record of 1,093. Texas A&M was second and Houston Baptist College third.

Houston's Bruce Ashworth was medalist with 212, 4 under, but he had to birdie the first two play-off holes against teammate Jim McLean for the honor. Third went to Cougar Corker DeLoach at 213.

Houston has now defeated 41 teams in seven tournaments this fall without a loss. However, Bruce Lietzke will be lost to the team for a month. He injured his right hand hitting a shot.

Ashworth beats me again.

AT LSU TOURNEY

Golfers stroke out team victory

By MIKE STACY
(Assistant Sports Editor)

Cougar golfers made it five wins in a row this year in tournament play as they won the 11th annual Louisiana State Invitational Golf Tournament by 20 strokes.

Paced by Jim McLean's two under par 282, the Cougars made shambles of the 11-team tournament.

Team captain Corker DeLoach finished in a second place tie with 284 as the defending NCAA champs shot a team total of 1,439.

McLean fired rounds of 69-69-72-72 to grab the individual title over the par 71, 6,365 yard LSU course.

Other Cougar scores included Tom Jenkins' 290, Bruce Lietzke's 291, John Mills' 292 and Buck Rogers' 295.

Southern Methodist finished a strong second behind Coach Dave Williams linksters.

The team totals were Houston, 1,439; SMU, 1,459; LSU and Georgia (tie), 1,461; North Texas State, 1,467; Florida State, 1,482; Memphis State, 1,495; Alabama, 1,497; Lamar Tech, 1,512; Ohio State, 1,546; University of Southwestern Louisiana, no score (did not field complete team).

My biggest win in college.

UH golfers capture 3 individual trophies

Three UH golfers, one an alumni and the other two still students, won golf tournaments this weekend.

Former UH star Babe Hiskey won the $100,000 Sahara Invitational Golf Tournament in Las Vegas, Nevada.

The victory meant $20,000 to the 31-year-old protege of Coach Dave Williams.

Williams said of Hiskey, "Babe never gave up, and I'm real proud of him and his wife."

UH sophomore Rick Belden, former Bellaire High graduate, won the men's city golf championship Sunday at Hermann Park when he shot a 282 for a three-stroke victory.

This was Belden's first win ever in a tournament.

The third Cougar to win this weekend was Jim McLean, who paced the Cougars to a 20-stroke win in the LSU Invitational last Saturday.

McLean won the individual title by two strokes, shooting rounds of 69-69-72-72.

"The way Jim has been shooting golf lately, he could be one of the best in the United States this year," Williams said.

My friend Rick Belden with a nice win.

McLean Paces Cougars

This was the year of brutal wind and a playoff for the individual title.

ALBUQUERQUE, N.M. — (AP) — Houston, behind the steady golf of Seattle's Jim McLean, opened up a 12-stroke lead yesterday after three rounds of the Tucker Intercollegiate golf tournament.

The Cougars, who have won the team title 12 years of the Tucker's 15-year existence, had a three-round total of 898. Arizona State jumped from fourth to second place yesterday, by-passing Brigham Young and Florida on the way, and had a three-round total of 910.

Florida, the first-round leader, continued its slide and wound up in fourth place after Friday's action. Brigham Young remained in third place.

McLean braved cool temperatures to fire a nifty one-under-par 71 over the 7,246-yard University of New Mexico golf course. The sub-par round gave McLean a 54-hole total of 221 shots.

Golf team's play pleases Williams

By STEVE PATE
(Sports Editor)

Sports writers are a strange breed of people who continuously look for the unusual story to draw reader interest.

But, alas, the time comes when one is forced to dip into the everyday happenings of a team—such as the UH golf team. It wins a lot, you know.

Have won 12 of 15

In fact, it wins nearly all the time. It's hard to find something different about a team that wins all the time. Twelve national titles in 15 years is a lot.

But wait. Maybe that's what makes it so different. It wins all the time. That's why Coach Dave Williams was honored this January as the greatest golf coach of all time.

And, don't be shocked, the UH golfers are winning again this year. They have won their first three outings. But now they may be tested.

"We have really been encouraged so far. Jim McLean and John Mills, who saw little action last year, are playing well," Williams said.

"Corker DeLoach is steady, Bruce Ashworth is having a slow start but he will catch on. He is not playing bad."

Wants competition

Then Coach Williams started talking about a coming tournament he would like to enter to really give the Cougars a test of heavy competition.

The tournament will be in Albuquerque, New Mexico, a 72-hole affair running from October 14 through 16. It will be called the Tucker Intercollegiate and will draw the likes of Brigham Young, which finished third in the NCAA tournament last year and returns all its starters.

Florida, Georgia, Wake Forest and LSU will also be there to supply enough competition to keep anybody interested. The only trouble for the Cougars will be getting there.

"We are going to try and work something out in our budget," Williams said. "I have an old car and we may be able to take it. But I'm not sure we can go."

"It's the first major tournament of the year and would give us a good idea of what we have," he added.

Six to compete

If the Cougars go, they will carry six golfers, Williams said. McLean, a junior from Seattle, Wash., and Mills, a junior from Portland, Maine, will team with Ashworth (All-America senior from Las Vegas), Tom Jenkins (senior from Houston Bellaire) and DeLoach (junior from McMinnville, Tenn.).

The sixth position will be decided in a tournament this week between Cougars Warren Kovar, freshman from Spring Branch; Stan Lee, freshman from Heber Springs, Ark.; Bruce Lietzke, sophomore from Beaumont; and Buck Rogers, from Texarkana, Tex.

Coach Williams's reports.

Jim McLean Wins Pacific Amateur

JIM McLEAN
... best in the west

Winning in San Francisco.

• **Jim McLean** of Seattle, Wash., won the Pacific Coast Amateur with 73-71-70-71—285, one stroke better than Barry Jaeckel of Los Angeles at the Olympic Club, San Francisco.

The University of Houston player began the final round two strokes behind Jaeckel, the third round leader, who closed with 74. Third was Gary Floan of Spokane, Wash., with 287, followed by Gary Sanders, Buena Park, Calif., with 290.

Sanders, former University of Southern California captain and college All-American, was the second round leader with 70-68—138, two strokes ahead of Floan and Jaeckel. McLean was six strokes off the pace at 144.

Jaeckel led after the first 18 holes with 67, followed by John Beetham of La Habra, Calif., with 68 and Alan Tapie of Downey, Calif., at 69.

285—Jim McLean, Seattle, Wash., 73-71-70-71.
286—Barry Jaeckel, Los Angeles, 67-73-72-74.
287—Gary Floan, Spokane, Wash., 71-69-74-73.
290—Gary Sanders, Buena Park, Calif., 70-68-77-75.
292—Artie McNickle, Sacramento, Calif., 72-75-74-71.
294—John Beetham, La Habra, Calif., 68-73-77-76; Bud Bradley, Los Angeles, 71-76-73-74; Pat Fitzsimons, Salem, Ore., 74-74-72-74.
296—Greg Trompas, San Diego, 75-75-72-74; Steve Cole, Seattle, Wash., 74-75-74-73; Ray Leach, Novato, Calif., 70-73-79-74; Aly Trompas, San Diego, 72-77-77-70.

(ABOVE LEFT) *Junior year in college.* (ABOVE RIGHT) *Check the sideburns.*

1970 PACIFIC NORTHWEST OPEN RESULTS

		Pro Money
*Jim McLean, Rainier G.&C.C.	284	
Bob Duden, Colwood G.C.	285	$2,500.00
Rick Jetter, San Jose, Calif.	286	1,750.00
Wayne Vollmer, Vancouver, B.C.	287	1,350.00
*Mike Davis, Riverside G.&C.C.	288	
*Pat Fitzsimons, Salem G.C.	288	
Bob McKendrick, Oswego Lake C.C.	289	1,005.00
Bill Eggers, Gresham G.&C.C.	289	1,005.00
Stan Leonard, Vancouver, B.C.	289	1,005.00
Bob Johnson, Fircrest G.C.	289	1,005.00
Boots Porterfield, Grants Pass G.C.	290	770.00
Jerry Mowlds, Riverside G.&C.C.	290	770.00
*Tom Tuell, Fircrest G.C.	291	
*Fred Haney, Rock Creek G.&C.C.	291	
Duane Bergstrom, Forest Hills C.C.	291	633.34
Tim Berg, Eugene C.C.	291	633.33
Bill Tindall, Longview C.C.	291	633.33
Ockie Eliason, Elks Allenmore G.C.	292	510.00
Tag Merritt, Meridian Valley C.C.	292	510.00
Bud Hofmeister, Hayden Lake, Idaho	292	510.00
*Dave Glenz, Coos C.C.	293	
Bob Litton, Vancouver, Wash.	293	390.00
Duke Matthews, Olympia G.&C.C.	293	390.00
Bill O'Brien, Renton Range	293	390.00
A/R-Bruce Cudd, Columbia-Edgewater C.C.	294	
Mike Dudik, Wing Point C.C.	294	305.00
Ed Bucklin, Moses Lake G.&C.C.	294	305.00
*Walt Christiansen, Capitol City G.C.	294	
*Chuck Milne, Salem G.C.	294	
Les Moe, Yakima G.&C.C.	295	245.00
Tom Liljeholm, Rose City G.C.	295	245.00
*Stu MacKenzie, Forest Hills C.C.	296	
*Kent Myers, Oswego Lake C.C.	296	
Ted Naff, Glendale C.C.	296	200.00
*Steve McDonald, Eastmoreland G.C.	297	
Bob Whisman, Everett Municipal G.C.	297	170.00
Ron Coleman, Dungeness G.&C.C.	297	170.00
Ron Hagen, Sand Point C.C.	298	126.67
Ted Wurtz, Tam O'Shanter G.C.	298	126.67
Tom Everham, Columbia Park G.C.	298	126.66
*Herm Mize, Indian Canyon G.C.	298	
Charles Leider, Burlingame, Calif.	299	120.00
*Craig Griswold, Oswego Lake C.C.	299	
*Gay Davis, Waverly C.C.	299	
*Bob Wolsborn, Gresham G.&C.C.	299	
Tom Boucher, Seattle	300	33.34
Mickey Shaw, Portland	300	33.33
Lloyd Harris, Suntides G.C.	300	33.33
*Bob Allard, Rock Creek C.C.	300	

*Denotes Amateur

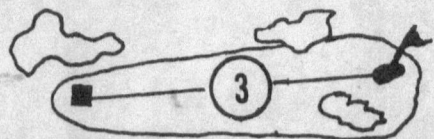

NO. 3 - 428 YARDS - PAR 4 Long, straight away hole. Length, out-of-bounds left and right, and large, sloping green make it one of the most difficult holes on the course.

Winning a professional tournament in Portland, Oregon, at age twenty-one.

1958

Team Members — Frank Wharton, Jim Hiskey, Phil Rodgers, Bob Pratt, Jacky Cupit, Richard Dickson, George Sykes, David Boies (Team was **undefeated.**)

TUCKER — New Mexico U. Golf Course, Albuquerque, New Mexico, 72 holes. Played in October of 1957, 54 holes (last 18 rained out). Jacky Cupit, 215; Frank Wharton, 216; Jim Hiskey, 221; Bob Pratt, 221.

BORDER OLYMPICS — Laredo, Texas, 36 holes. Phil Rodgers, 67-70—137; Richard Dickson, 67-74—141; Frank Wharton, 72-70—142; Jim Hiskey, 72-71—143. Total of 563 (13 under par . . . a new record).

ALL AMERICA — Pine Forest C. C., 72 holes, Houston. Overall Champions (Jacky Cupit, David Boies, Jim Hiskey and Frank Wharton).
Team Medal Play Champions — Cupit, 289; Hiskey, 296; Boies, 303; Wharton, 306.
Team Low Four Ball Champions — 260 — (Cupit, Boies, Wharton and J. Hiskey.)
Team Low Two Ball Champions — 275 — (Cupit, Boies).
Team Match Play Champions — (Cupit, Boies, Hiskey, Wharton).

BEAUMONT ENTERPRISE — Tyrell Park Golf Course, Beaumont, Texas — 36 holes. Hiskey, 136 (8 under par); Wharton, 137; Pratt, 143; and George Sykes, 148. Team total 564 (12 under par).

EAST TEXAS — Jasper Country Club, Jasper, Texas, 36 holes. Pratt, 141; J. Hiskey, 142; Wharton, 142; Boies, 143; and Cupit, 145.

MISSOURI VALLEY CONFERENCE — Wichita C. C., Wichita, Kansas — 54 holes. Phil Rodgers, 215; Pratt, 216; Hiskey, 223; Wharton, 231.

NCAA CHAMPIONSHIPS — Taconic Golf Club, Williamstown, Mass., 36 holes. Phil Rodgers, 139; Jim Hiskey, 142; Jacky Cupit, 143; Frank Wharton, 146; Bob Pratt 146; Team total 570 (6 under par . . . a new NCAA Record).

FRANK WHARTON — Fall, 1954-Spring, 1958. Home: Dallas, Texas. Played on three National Championship teams, 1956, 1957 and 1958. Played on three Missouri Valley Conference Championship Teams, 1956, 1957, 1958. Selected on NCAA Coaches All American Team 1958 (first year All America teams were selected in golf). Won 1956 West Texas Relays. Won 1957 Border Olympics. Finished 2nd in 1956 All America and third in 1957. Finished 4th in Medal Play in NCAA in 1957. Went to Quarterfinals in NCAA in 1958. Won Texas PGA Championship with sensational eagle 2 on last hole (held an 8 iron for the deuce) in 1957. Runner-up in Tucker in fall of 1957. Played on numerous Championship Teams at UH. Member of three All America Championship Teams 1956, 1957 and 1958.

JIM HISKEY — Fall, 1954-Spring, 1958. Home: Pocatello, Idaho. Member of three All America Championship Teams, 1956, 1957 and 1958. Member of three Missouri Valley Conference Championship Teams, 1956, 1957, 1958. Selected on NCAA Golf Coaches All America Team 1958. Won All America in 1957. Finished 3rd in Southern Intercollegiates in 1958 at Athens, Ga. Low Amateur in Tam O'Shanter in 1957. Won Charles Saunders Award (UH Award for Sportsmanship, Leadership and Scholarship for all Senior Athletes). Won Beaumont Enterprise Intercollegiate 1958. Quarterfinalist in 1956 NCAA Championships. Tied for third in 1958 All America and finished 4th in 1956 All America. Placed 5th in NCAA Medal Play in 1958. Member of many UH Team Championships and won many Invitational tournaments and placed well in many tournaments such as the Trans, Southern, and State Championships. Won Idaho State Amateur and Utah State Amateur Championships while at UH. Won Idaho State Amateur Championship three straight years.

PHIL RODGERS (Fall, 1956-Fall, 1958). Home: LaJolla, Calif. Won NCAA Championship in 1958. Won Missouri Valley Conference 1958. Won Border Olympics in 1958. Played in Masters while at UH. Quarterfinalist in National Amateur . . . lost to Rex Baxter. Co-Medalist in NCAA in 1958. Selected on NCAA Golf Coaches All America Team for 1958. Co-Medalist in Western Amateur 1958 (72 holes).

Left to right: Jacky Cupit, Phil Rodgers, Jim Hiskey, Coach Dave Williams, Frank Wharton and Bob Pratt.

he dynasty begins.

1962 ALL AMERICA CHAMPIONS: Fred Marti, Homero Blancas, Coach Dave Williams, Babe Hiskey and Kermit Zarley.

MIDDLE LEFT: Wright Garrett sinks his birdie putt on 18 during the 1963 All America. MIDDLE RIGHT: Kermit Zarley on his way to setting the All America Record in 1963. He shot 280 (8 under par). BOTTOM LEFT: 1962 Tucker Champs. Standing: Harry Toscano, Fred Marti, Kermit Zarley, Mark Hopkins. Kneeling: Wright Garrett, Ted Hale.

Four future PGA Tour players and Coach Williams.

I missed Picture Day.

UH 1970 GOLF TEAM
Standing: Bruce Ashworth, Corker DeLoach, John Mahaffey, Joe Stencik, Kip Puterbaugh, Tom Jenkins. Kneeling: Bobby Walzel, Bruce Lietzke, John Grace, John Cameron, and John Mills.

1970

Team Members — John Mahaffey, Corker DeLoach, Bruce Ashworth, Tom Jenkins, John Mills, Kip Puterbaugh, Jim McLean, Bruce Lietzke, Bobby Walzel, Arthur Russell, Joe Stencik, Bobby Wadkins, John Grace, Bill Rogers, Layne Wallock.

Bruce Ashworth after he sank his 3 foot birdie putt on the 72nd hole of the 1969 All America.

KIP PUTERBAUGH — Fall, 1965-Spring, 1970. Home: La Jolla, Calif. Won the Bill Shelton 1969 (fall). Won the Sterling Hogan, Jr. 1969. Member of the Centenary Championship Team 1969 (fall). Member of 1970 L. R. Goldman Championship Team. Member of Bill Shelton and Sterling Hogan Championship Teams in 1969. Member of Tucker Championship Team in fall of 1969. Southern California Champion 1968.

1969 ALL AMERICA CHAMPIONS
Bob Barbarossa, John Mahaffey, Doug Olson, Bruce Ashworth.

John Mahaffey

Bruce Ashworth

Coach Williams

Dave Shuster

Doug Olson

Bob Barbarossa

1969 NCAA CHAMPIONS

"How Sweet It Is" . . . UH wins 1969 All America.

30

I caddied for Ashworth in this tournament.

UH Athletic Director Harry Fouke at 1970 All America Pre-Tournament Banquet.

JOHN MAHAFFEY — Fall, 1966-Spring, 1970. Home: Kerrville, Texas. Played on two National Championship Teams in 1969 and 1970. Played on 1969 All America Championship Team. Won NCAA in 1970. Finished 11th in 1969 NCAA. Won L. R. Goldman in 1968. Won Pikes Peak Intercollegiate 1968. Won El Dorado Intercollegiate 1968 (fall). Won Les Bolstad in 1969. Won Lake Charles Intercollegiate in 1969. Won LSU Intercollegiate in 1969. Won Atascocita Intercollegiate 1969. Runner-up in Guy Savage Intercollegiate in 1968 and 1969 (fall). Runner-up in Forest Cove Intercollegiate in 1968. Runner-up in Atascocita 1970. Runner-up in Northern Intercollegiate 1969 (fall). Runner-up in Bill Shelton 1968 (fall). Semifinalist in Western Amateur 1970.

KEN NEWELL — Fall, 1966-Spring, 1970. Home: Ft. Worth, Texas. Played on 1969 Atascocita Championship Team. Member of 1968 (fall) Guy Savage Championship Team.

DAVE SHUSTER — Fall, 1967-Spring, 1970. Home: Juno Beach, Florida. Member of 1968 (fall) and 1969 (fall) Centenary Team Championships. Member of 1968 (fall) Guy Savage Championship Team. Member of the Buckeye Intercollegiate Championship Team 1969 (fall). Runner-up in Buckeye Championship 1969 (fall). Member of 1968 (fall) El Dorado Championship Team. Runner-up in 1968 (fall) El Dorado. Runner-up in Southern Amateur in 1969. Member of 1968 Lake Charles Championship Team. Member of L. R. Goldman Championship Team in 1969. Member of LSU (New Orleans) championship team 1969 (fall). Member of Northern Intercollegiate Championship Team 1969 (fall). Member of Pikes Peak Championship Team 1968. Member of Bill Shelton Championship Teams of 1968 and 1969. Member of 1968 Sun Devil Championship. Member of 1968 Les Bolstad Championship Team.

Coach Dave Williams, Bruce Ashworth, Corker DeLoach, John Mahaffey, John Mills. Tournament was played on the Scarlet Course at Ohio State University, Columbus, Ohio. The Cougars also won their first National Championship here in 1956.

We beat Wake Forest by two shots.

Nice picture of Don Scott—from a famous Texas ant story.

DON SCOTT

I'm in the sunglasses behind Coach Williams.

From the 1970 Northwest Open.

McLean Powers Houston to Lead In Tucker Play

By BOB RUSSO

Behind Jim McLean's one-under-par 71, the University of Houston began to widen its lead in the third round of the 16th annual William H. Tucker Invitational Collegiate Golf Tournament at the weather-toughened University South course Friday.

Bundled in a thick sweater, and with a ski cap over his ears, McLean easily conquered the 7246-yard, par-72 University layout, which along with bitter cold weather has harassed scores. His 71 Friday, combined with previous rounds of 74 and 76 gave him a 221 total for 54 holes and a one shot individual lead over Dennis Walters of North Texas State.

Houston's team total of 898 left runnerup Arizona State (910) and Brigham Young (912) far behind with only today's round left.

In the college division, Odessa College took the lead over U.S. International, the defending champ, with a 949 total compared to USI's 980 mark. Texas Wesleyan was third at a far 1020.

INDIVIDUALLY USI'S Pat McDonald breezed through play Friday with a 75 for a 236 total, a shot ahead of Odessa's Larry Malone, Pat O'Donnell and Scott Stegner. The fourth Odessa player, Wade Hudman was alone in third place with a 238 total.

Defending women's champion Cathy Caughan of Arizona State carded a medalist score of 78 Friday for a 123 total and the gals lead. Cathy had a 45 for Thursday's nine-hole round.

With Jan Schult at 128, a second place total, ASU leads the team standings with a 251 total over Odessa's 273 mark.

DEFENDING UNIVERSITY champion Ray Leach of Brigham Young finished play Friday with a one-under 71 for a 223 total and third place.

Dan Sheff of Arizona State and Bruce Ashworth of Houston shared Friday's low round with superb three-under-par 69's. Ashworth, during the round, eagled the tough 612-yard, par-5, ninth hole.

Another eagle, by Mike Killian of Florida, who had one of three opening day 69's, was recorded on the 466-yard, 10th hole. Other first round leaders Andy North of Florida and Bob Shallenberger of Arizona were at 225 and 227 respectively after play Friday.

New Mexico State's Bruce McKenzie carved out an even-par 72 Friday to go along with his 74 and 80 for a 226 total. Dave Newquist was the University of New Mexico's low golfer with rounds of 72-81-75 for a 228 total.

Probably the worst weather I ever played in. I eventually lost the playoff to Bruce Lietzke, Dennis Walters, and Ray Leach.

JIM MCLEAN . . . Defending champion from Seattle's Rainier Country Club has learned well as Houston University linksman . . . Outstanding chipper, and inured to wind by years in Texas, he could repeat.

BOB DUDEN . . . Glendoveer veteran has best record in PNW Section over past 25 years . . . Has won every major title in Section, except Pay Less . . . Currently holds PNW PGA and Oregon Open crowns . . . was Low Pro in '70 PNW Open . . . Tied for second in '70 Pay Less Classic . . . One of the finest wood players in history of golf.

DON BIES . . . Currently on tour and playing well. This sweet swinger will be tagged the favorite.

TED NAFF . . . Seattle assistant recently won Washington PGA crown . . . One of Section's finest young players, he has remarkable "touch" with wedge and putter . . . Could be a top contender at Ocean Shores.

1971 . . . Year of the Pro?

The kids, bless their flat stomachs, long hair and tender years, have been having their innings on the Pacific Northwest golf scene. On July 28, when the 1971 Northwest Open champion is crowned, a golfer with a hole in his haircut, a tight belt and professional intent could ascend the victory podium.

Defending champion at Ocean Shores is Jim McLean, the Seattle towhead who in recent years has been studying eagles and birdies at University of Houston. In 1969, the title went to Pat Fitzsimons, the Salem teen-age whiz. Not since 1968, when Portland veteran Bob Duden picked off his third Open crown, have the professionals subdued the impertinent amateurs.

The pros, however, are beginning to become peturbed. Not only have the kids been collecting the major Open crowns in the Section, but they have been ganging up to pummel their teachers in the annual Hudson Cup matches. Experience, seniority and pride being what they are, the amateur set could get its lumps at Ocean Shores.

One of the strongest professional fields in the history of the tournament is set to fire at the college set. Touring performers such as Don Bies, Al Mengert and Jerry Mowlds, backed by a host of outstanding club professionals, including Duden, Jim Petersen, Boots Porterfield, Tom Liljeholm, Bob Johnson, Mike Davis, Al Feldman, Bob McKendrick, Ted Naff and Duke Matthews, give the pros reason to foresee a return to normalcy.

Until Fitzsimons won at Inglewood Country Club in '69, a full decade had gone by with the professionals solidly in charge of the Open. This was bad enough, but McLean had to add insult to injury by nosing out Duden by a shot last year at Columbia-Edgewater. Not since the late Bud Ward zipped the pros in 1946-48 has an amateur's name been inscribed three consecutive years on the ancient Open plaque.

A professional victory would appear a solid wager —provided the collegians keep in mind the fact respect for their elders is a virtue.

5

LIFE ON THE LINKS

The Legend of Homero's 55

Before my time at the University of Houston, Homero Blancas was a name we all came to know very well on our golf team. After all, he was in *Ripley's Believe It or Not!* for the incredible performance he turned in one day in Longview, Texas.

Homero was already doing great on the PGA Tour by the time I got to Houston. During his college and amateur career, Homero had been considered the most talented amateur in America. But in the early 1960s, while still at Houston, he set a record so astonishing, it still echoes through the halls of golf history: He shot the lowest recorded round ever—55. In a tournament!

I had the chance to sit down with Homero during a pro–am we played in Longview (which, for those unfamiliar, is a place as flat as a pancake left on a Texas griddle in July). It's right off I-20 where, years later, I would receive a speeding ticket and was then taken directly before a magistrate in a courtroom. I had to pay the fine on the spot. No fooling around in Longview. Anyway, over a plate of fried chicken and an iced tea, Homero gave me the full details of his 55, straight from the man himself.

It was the fourth round of a tournament at Longview Country Club, a par-70 course definitely known more for its wind and tumbleweeds than its glamour. Homero wasn't even close to the lead in that tournament going into the final day. That honor belonged to Fred Marti, another UH teammate and an exceptional player in his own right.

Fred had a ten-shot lead on the field, and let's just say that most folks thought the tournament was as good as over. Fred's father, the head professional at Houston's Memorial Park, was confident in his son's victory, telling Fred to call him before he left for the drive back to Houston. He wanted Fred to give him the winning margin—before leaving Longview. No cell phones in 1960.

Homero teed off that morning of the tournament with no expectations of rewriting the record books. But, as the round unfolded, something magical started happening:

- A couple of birdies out of the gate.
- An eagle on the seventh hole, putting him at 4-under.
- Back-to-back birdies on eight and nine.

That's a 29 on the front nine, folks. Lightning in a bottle is taking form.

Then came the back nine, where Homero's round turned into the stuff of legend.

"I just kept hitting it close," he told me, shrugging as if shooting a 55 was no big deal. "And then the putts kept dropping."

He birdied ten, eleven, twelve. Boom—another eagle on thirteen. Now he's at 10-under. Several people hearing about the 29 had started following Homero. The folks watching started whispering about something very special happening.

- Birdie on fourteen.
- Eagle on the par-5 fifteenth.

At this point, Homero was in the zone known to a very small group of sports legends. The golf gods were most definitely smiling down on him. And he did not let up. As all golfers know, when you have a career round going, it's natural to play safe on the last few holes to preserve a great score. Not Homero.

- Birdie on sixteen.
- A par on seventeen (even legends have to breathe).
- And, finally, a birdie on eighteen to close it out.

That's 15-under-par for the day and a final score of 55!

Meanwhile, Fred Marti wasn't exactly lying down. He carded a very solid 66 in the final round—a score that should have won easily, especially in the fourth round. But even a stellar 66 isn't enough when your opponent shoots 55. It was so ironic that Fred lost the tournament by one stroke after starting the day with a 10-shot lead—seemingly impossible!

But the real Texas-sized punchline came when Fred called his dad back in Houston, just before leaving. Of course, from a pay phone.

"How much did you win by, Fred?" his father asked.

"I didn't win," Fred replied.

There was a long pause. "Damn it, Fred," his dad finally barked. "What did you shoot, an 80?"

Fred sighed. "No, I shot 66 . . . but Homero shot 55."

Dead silence on the other end of the line. What could you say? Your son played a great round, only to lose to the greatest round in golf history.

Homero's 55 was an official tournament round on a par-70 course, but it's still the lowest recorded round in history. To this day, it stands as a testament to what's possible when you're teeing off with almost no chance of victory.

And Fred? Well, he's a legend, too—just for a very different reason.

Billy Ray Brown Goes to See Jackie Burke

Billy Ray Brown was Texas through and through—rugged, handsome, and super talented. He was one of the greatest players in Houston Cougar history, and anyone who watched him swing a golf club could see why. With a driver in hand, Billy Ray was a machine. His irons were precise, his ball-striking exquisite. He could carve shots through the wind, pierce tight fairways, and stick it to the pin like nobody's business.

But putting? Oh, putting was his Achilles' heel. While Billy Ray wasn't terrible, he wasn't good either—just adequate. And "adequate" didn't cut it in Coach Dave Williams's book, especially when you were as gifted as Billy Ray in every other part of the game.

Coach, always a step ahead, decided it was time for Billy Ray to get a real lesson in putting. Who better to help than Jackie Burke, cofounder of the legendary Champions Golf Club and one of the greatest putters of all time? Jackie was a former Masters and PGA Champion, a tenacious Marine, and a man whose teaching style could best be described as "unapologetically blunt." Coach figured if anyone could fix Billy Ray's putting woes, it was Jackie Burke.

Champions Golf Club wasn't just any course. It was a shrine to golf, a place where legends lived. The club had hosted many major championships, and its two founders, Jimmy Demaret and Jackie Burke, were Masters champions in their own right. Jimmy had three green jackets.

When Billy Ray arrived at Champions, he was full of hope but also a touch of Texas swagger. He met Jackie on the putting green and wasted no time explaining his struggles with short putts.

"I'm having trouble with the putts inside six feet," said Billy Ray. Burke, always direct, listened for about a minute before taking charge.

Jackie led Billy Ray to a four-foot breaking putt—exactly the type of putt he might be having trouble with. "Alright," Jackie said, "Let's see what you've got."

Billy Ray took his stance, made a weak stroke, and pulled the ball just left of the hole. Jackie nodded, motioned for him to try again. On the second attempt, Billy Ray left it short. The third went wide right. On the fourth try, he pulled the ball left again.

Before the ball even stopped rolling, Jackie's right hand shot out like a piston and smacked Billy Ray square on the side of the head. It wasn't a light tap, either—it was a Marine-grade blow. The kind that left no room for interpretation. Billy Ray stumbled back, stunned, his face a mix of shock and indignation.

"Why'd you do that?!" Billy Ray asked, rubbing his head and staring at Jackie like he'd just been sucker punched in a bar fight.

Jackie's expression didn't change. He looked Billy Ray dead in the eye and said, "Because I want you to feel pain when you miss a short putt, Billy Ray."

The message landed harder than the slap. Jackie wasn't there to coddle anyone. He wanted Billy Ray to understand that missed short putts weren't just errors—they were personal failures and affronts to the game itself.

Billy Ray may have left Champions that day with a sore head, but he also left with a new understanding of the mental and physical stakes of putting. Jackie Burke wasn't just teaching technique; he was teaching accountability, the kind that sticks with you long after the sting fades.

To this day, that story has become a part of Houston Cougar golf lore and well-known on the PGA Tour too. It serves as a reminder that, sometimes, the toughest lessons are the ones that truly make you better. And Billy Ray did improve his short putting a bit after that, but at least he knew one thing for sure: He never wanted to miss in front of Jackie Burke again.

Billy Ray Brown would win the individual NCAA Championship and go on to have a successful PGA Tour career, including three wins, and then a successful career in broadcasting. You can still see him regularly now on The Golf Channel telecasts.

Divots

One afternoon, I was practicing with my roommate Bruce Lietzke, watching him hit his usual effortless and powerful fades. But something was bothering me. His divots were flying way too far left. I mean, they weren't just a little left; they looked like they were trying to exit stage left and back to Baldwin House.

I mentioned it to Bruce. "You know your divots are going massively left?"

Bruce, never one to overcomplicate things, took another swing, glanced at the ground for about half a second, and shrugged. "I guess so."

That was it. No concern, no second thoughts. Meanwhile, I was standing there trying to solve the mystery like a detective in a crime novel. A problem I would have as a player but something that would absolutely help me as a teacher/coach.

Besides the divots, I knew Bruce had a backswing that went way inside. I knew the clubface was closed and that he had a noticeable sway away from the ball in his takeaway, his left wrist bowed at the top and his arms looped out (a lot) on the downswing. But somehow, he hit continuous long, high baby fades—every single time. It was mind-blowing.

Those divots haunted me. I wanted answers. I dug deeper.

"What about that bowed left wrist?" I asked, hoping to at least get him to acknowledge some part of his bizarrely effective swing.

Bruce didn't hesitate with his answer. "What do you want the wrist to look like at impact?"

I thought for a second and said, "Slightly bowed."

He nodded. "Well, I already have that." And that was the end of that discussion.

I wasn't ready to give up. "Let's revisit the divots going so far left."

Bruce just shrugged again. "I don't really look at the divots." Conversation over.

And that was Bruce in a nutshell—zero overthinking or concern for what anything looked like, and, somehow, the results were always perfect. Meanwhile, I was left standing there, questioning everything I thought I knew at that time about the golf swing.

Looking back, all those years playing with Bruce had a massive impact on my teaching career. At the time, I didn't realize I was getting a front-row education in what really matters in a golf swing—what the ball is doing! Later on, when I wrote *The X-Factor Swing* and *The Eight-Step Swing*, a lot of what I had learned from Bruce found its way into my teaching.

I listened to many teachers through the years—as I studied the great ball-strikers—and realized many ideas they expounded were not correct. Especially how many great players swing the club much farther around and left than most understood. I eventually wrote a cover piece in the 1980s: "SWING LEFT TO SWING RIGHT"—Thank you, Bruce Lietzke!

There certainly is no one perfect swing, and there is no one perfect method. Many well-known teachers would've changed a young Bruce Lietzke, which would've been a disaster. I have been extremely careful when I see a talented young player with a different-looking golf swing. My mantra: "Do no harm!"

Caddies: The Unsung Heroes

All of us in Houston had to caddie or do something productive during the All-American Intercollegiate, which was the crème de la crème of college golf. This wasn't just another tournament; it was *the* tournament. It had more star power than a Tom Cruise thriller, second only to the NCAA Championship. For us, it was home turf, and with it came all the pressure of defending our title against the best teams in the country. But let me tell you, there was nothing like having a great caddie to lighten the load, keep you sharp, and make the experience unforgettable.

Three years before, in my freshman year, I had the privilege of looping for Bruce Ashworth, and I swear I picked up more pointers from caddying for him than any practice round could've taught me. But this time, I want to tell you about Van Gillen. In 1972, during my senior year, Van caddied for me in the All-American, and let me tell you, he was more than a caddie. He was a one-man pep rally, a course strategist, and a part-time comedian rolled into one.

Van wasn't your typical caddie. No, sir. He attacked the job with the enthusiasm of a West Texas oil prospector striking black gold. From the moment we stepped onto the course, he had a game plan. The guy had the entire layout of the course mapped out, almost like he was getting ready to launch a lunar landing. And whatever I did—good, bad, or ugly—Van reacted like it was part of some master plan he'd cooked up in his head.

When I rolled in a putt, especially on the last day when the stakes were higher, Van didn't just celebrate. He *performed*. Picture this: Van Gillen dancing around the green, holding the flagstick like it was a victory torch at the Olympics. He was like a cowboy at the rodeo, and it was downright contagious. Even the other teams couldn't help but chuckle, though I'm sure they were shaking their heads, wondering if we'd completely lost our minds.

Throughout the week, Van didn't miss a beat. He was sharp as a rattlesnake's fang when it came to reading greens, and he had a sixth sense about club selection. Not only did his knowledge make a difference, his attitude did as well. He had this way of making everything feel lighter. I could have hit a poor shot, missing a green by a wide margin, and he'd spin it into a joke about how "all great players need an unlikely great up-and-down."

Van had a knack for keeping me loose, and that was no small thing when you're carrying the weight of defending a title at your home event. The pressure? Oh, it was thicker than Texas humidity in August. But, with Van, it was like having a stand-up comedian and a sports psychologist in your corner.

On the last day of the tournament, I played some of the best golf of my college career without winning. I finished fifth individually, and our team took home the trophy for the second year in a row. Sure, I hit the shots, but I'll tell you straight: It was Van Gillen who made it possible. His energy, his preparation, and his ability to keep me relaxed were the secret sauce.

The lesson here? A great caddie does more than just carry your bag. They might carry the day. And if they can make you laugh while doing it, all the better. Golf is a game, after all, and it's meant to be fun. Van reminded me of that in the best way possible.

To all the players out there, don't underestimate the power of a top-tier caddie. They might just be the difference between a good round and a great one—and between a stressful day and one you'll never forget.

Oh, and one more thing. If your caddie starts dancing on the green like he's at a honky-tonk, just let him. Sometimes, you've got to let the show steal itself.

6

TIPS FROM THE TOP

Galveston

One of the luckiest things in my life was becoming friends with Jackie Burke at the famous Champions Golf Club in Houston. Well, of course, I wasn't "friends" with Mr. Burke back in college, but I did get to meet him very early, during my freshman year. One of my teammates, Rick Belden, was from Houston and a member there, and we got along well. Every so often, Rick would take me out to Champions, where I also got to meet Jimmy Demaret. Jimmy, mind you, had won the Masters three times, and Jackie Burke—well, he had also won the Masters, plus the PGA Tour. He'd also led the PGA money list and played on five Ryder Cup teams.

For some reason, Jackie took an interest in me early on. Whenever I could, I'd slip into his office just to ask him questions, take notes, and listen to him talk. And, boy, Jackie had phenomenal insights. He had advice and opinions on just about everything. I hung on every word, and I quickly realized that this man was going to be a huge influence in my life.

One of the encounters I had with Jackie Burke became a famous story in golf circles. Here's the Galveston story: It was my junior year, and I was set to play in the Masters. In 1971, I'd finished fourth in the US Amateur, which earned me an exemption into Augusta. Naturally, I was a little on edge with the big event just a couple months away. So, one day, I was out at Champions and spotted Jackie. I mentioned I was having some trouble with my driving and, with the Masters right around the corner, asked if he had a tip for me.

Without missing a beat, he looked at me and said, "Take three golf balls down to Galveston and hit them out into the Gulf of Mexico." Then he turned around and walked off. Just like that.

I was sure he was blowing me off, maybe messing with me a bit. I wasn't about to drive fifty miles down to Galveston to hit a few balls into the ocean.

But then, as fate would have it, a few weeks later, two of my teammates and I decided to drive down to Galveston to hang out. Galveston's the kind of place where you drive your car right onto the beach and walk around town. If you've ever been there, you know that the Galveston beach is not Miami Beach. Far from it. The sand is rock-hard—practically pavement. That's why you can drive on it. Anyway, as we were walking over to get something to eat, the thought of hitting three balls into the Gulf of Mexico crossed my mind. My clubs were in the trunk of my '64 Chevy Convertible (which, as a point of interest, I had bought for six hundred dollars), so I figured, *Why not?*

I grabbed my driver and three balls, walked down to the beach, found a spot, teed up three balls in that firm sand, and launched those balls into the gulf. But to be very honest, this didn't mean a thing to me.

About a week later, I was back at Champions, and saw Jackie on the driving range. I walked over to him and said, "I did what you told me."

He looked at me, clearly not remembering, and asked, "What did I tell you?" Was he serious? Or was he testing me? Hard to say with Jackie.

I told him I'd taken three balls down to Galveston and hit them into the Gulf of Mexico. He nodded, as if remembering, and said, "Oh, yes, and what did you learn?"

I stood there, feeling like he was playing me again. But I had to answer him. I said, "I didn't learn anything."

He looked at me with that sharp gaze of his and asked, "Well, how did you hit them?"

"Well," I said, "I think I hit them all excellent—right out of the center of the clubface."

Then Jackie gave me one of those famous Burke looks. "Well, that's it, you dumb son of a bitch. The secret is you don't aim at anything. Just swing like you're hitting it into the Gulf of Mexico. You understand? You can't miss it."

And, with that, he turned and walked off.

I stood there for a minute, letting it sink in. I had to admit, I'd hit those balls as well as I possibly could. Turns out it was a fantastic lesson. When I got into a tough driving situation, I'd recall Jackie Burke's lesson. It was a great one! And it's something I've taught my students ever since. Don't aim the driver or try to steer it. Instead, make a full, let-go swing. Trust me, you will be a far better driver.

More Jackie Burke Advice

One week before I was leaving to play in the Masters in 1972, I was out playing at Champions with some team members. We were playing Cypress that day, which is the course used for the US Open and Ryder Cup matches. It's the more famous of the two great golf courses at Champions.

I spotted Jackie Burke and knew this was definitely the last time I'd see him before going to Augusta. I walked over and asked him for one last tip. *Mr. Burke, what do you think I should be thinking on that first tee shot?*

Without skipping a beat, he said, "Take the longest backswing of your life." As always, his answer came immediately, with no thinking.

I did think for a moment before I responded. "Why would I do that?"

Jackie said, "So you can at least get the club halfway back." It was a very short and concise answer, and he spun and left right away.

Take the longest backswing of my life? This thought didn't make any sense to me. So I pretty much just forgot about it.

That is until I was standing on the tee at the Masters, with about ten thousand people lining both sides of the fairway, congregating around the first tee and near the putting green and near the ninth green and near the eighteenth green. It was just a mass of people. Anyone who's been to Augusta knows what I'm talking about.

I had a 2:25 p.m. tee time, so I'd been up all day, waiting for this moment. It was safe to say that anyone who had ever played in the Masters will never forget their first tee shot. This would include Jack Nicklaus or Tiger Woods or Rory McIlroy. I know everyone playing in the Masters, for their first time, remembers this tee shot. In the first round, I'm paired with the PGA Champion Al Geiberger. He was considered to have the smoothest and maybe best golf swing on the tour.

At the Masters, they kept things quite simple for the first tee shot, but one thing they did was slide your name into a stanchion on the back of that tee box before you hit. It was pretty surreal to see my name go up. Al was hitting first, and I was definitely expecting a perfect tee shot from this highly respected veteran. But, to my amazement, he hit a snap hook into the left trees. It was a terrible shot. And with that, for some reason, I relaxed about one hundred times more than I was one second before. Still, I was tremendously nervous as I teed up my golf ball. Just at that moment, I remembered Jackie Burke's advice—*Take the longest backswing of your life*—and that was exactly what I did. I'm sure it wasn't the longest swing in my life, but I had a perfect drive. To be honest, I don't remember swinging at all, but it sure was great seeing that ball going straight down the middle of the fairway.

I went on to make the cut, which was a nice thing in my life. Al Geiberger and I became friends, and whenever I saw him anywhere, I would always put my arm around him and thank him for that snap hook. We would both have a laugh! It was probably the worst opening tee shot Al had ever hit anywhere, anytime in his life. I don't think anything else could have relaxed me more in that moment. Thanks to Al's snap hook and Jackie's advice, I got off that first tee at the Masters. And I've remembered that moment—and that "long backswing"—ever since.

Pick Them Up

One thing that would definitely surprise today's golfers is that at Houston we actually picked up our own golf balls after hitting them on the range. That's right—no ball-picker machines or free buckets of balls. Just us, our clubs, and a whole lot of retrieving.

Back then, not many golf courses even had ranges, and if they did, they charged by the bucket. Most of us didn't exactly have pockets full of extra cash, so paying for balls was more of a luxury than a regular practice routine. Instead, we'd hit our own balls, then go collect them, being as careful as possible not to have them too far apart because, trust me, no one wanted to be zigzagging all over a field on a golf ball hunt, wasting time and energy. Often, we would pick them up and hit another three or four more bags, with each shag bag holding up to one hundred balls—the balls we had used ourselves.

One of our main go-to spots was at the Houston Executive Club, formerly the old Houston Country Club before it moved to another part of town. Now, the club is one of the finest (and wealthiest) clubs in the country. But the old Exec was still a very nice course, and the practice field had a couple bunkers where we could work on our bunker shots. It was the perfect place for college players to hit and then pick up their shag balls.

When you have to pick up your own golf balls, it's amazing how accurate you suddenly become. Every shot you hit with specific clubs made your aiming much more precise. You definitely tried to hit those balls as close together as possible.

Professionals are naturally good at this; they're trained to notice where every ball lands. The modern-day pro has a Trackman or Foresight launch monitor, tracking every shot most days.

But watching amateurs these days hitting free-range balls, spraying balls all over the place, I wish I could have them hit their own balls for a few months and see how much better they become. They wouldn't be so careless if they had to walk it out there and collect them afterward. If everyone today had to pick up their own balls, they'd pay more attention to where each one landed, and they'd start noticing their own "scatter pattern"—how well they controlled distance and how wide their shots spread from side to side. After a few weeks of this, I guarantee you'd see improvement. Nothing motivates a golfer much more than looking for their own golf balls.

At the University of Houston, picking up balls was an art form. And speaking of artistry, we all became experts at scooping them up with a sand wedge. There was a skill to sliding the club under the ball, popping it up with a few controlled bounces, and landing it right into the shag bag. At Houston, we could all fill a shag bag in no time.

Most people have seen that iconic Tiger Woods commercial, where he bounces the ball off his club, behind his back, through his legs, then up high before smashing it down the range. But trust me, we had guys at Houston doing similar tricks long before Tiger's time. It's amazing what practice—and the need to avoid extra trips across a field—can teach you.

The Underwood Theory

Hal Underwood was a legend in amateur golf—the number one amateur in the United States. The guy could flat-out play, and everyone knew it. But, despite his almost mythical status, Hal wasn't strutting around campus with an entourage. Nope, he was back for a fifth year at Houston, not to chase glory but to do something far less glamorous: Graduate! We played so much golf and traveled to so many tournaments, it was extremely difficult to graduate in four years.

I didn't see much of Hal around Baldwin House, where we all resided. He had his own orbit, and most of us weren't in it. But every once in a while, I'd catch him out at the Executive Golf Course, better known as Exec. It was a place where we had a wide-open field and ample room to hit every club in the bag, but, of course, you had to pick them up. Exec wasn't at all fancy, now serving as a public golf course. Hal could've played at any exclusive club in Houston—and probably had a standing invitation at most of them—but there he was at Exec, hitting his own balls like some blue-collar golf savant. It was like seeing a thoroughbred racehorse hanging out at a pony ride.

One day, I was out there, too, hammering away at my shag balls. At times, I felt like I was making pretty good progress. Then I noticed Hal, effortlessly striping ball after ball in a methodical rhythm. Curious, I shuffled over to say hello and ask a few questions.

"Hal," I said, wiping the sweat off my brow, "what's your secret to hitting balls out here?"

He paused, casually leaned on his 4-iron, and gave me what I would come to know as the "Underwood Theory."

"You wanna know something?" he drawled in that smooth Texas cadence that made you feel like every word he said should be written down in a bible. "When I hit five hundred golf balls—which I do pretty often—I've noticed this: The first three are good, and the last three are good. Everything in between? Not so much."

And just like that, the Underwood Theory was born. Short, sweet, and as Texas as a pair of worn cowboy boots—understated brilliance with a little dust on it.

Then he shrugged, tossed his club over his shoulder, and moseyed off to pick up his shots, leaving me standing there in stunned silence. He didn't explain it, didn't elaborate, didn't ask for feedback. He just dropped that nugget of wisdom like it was gospel and left me to chew on it. What was it?

Now, what are we supposed to learn from this? On the surface, it sounded like a riddle a wise old cowboy might tell you while fixing a fence—profound, mysterious, and just cryptic enough to make you question your own intelligence. But here's the deal: Hal wasn't wrong.

Apparently, when you hit balls for hours on end, your brain plays tricks on you. The first three shots? Those are pure because you're relaxed and not overthinking things. But then the devil creeps in—the temptation to tinker with your grip, adjust your stance, or "fix" something in your swing that probably wasn't broken to begin with. And that's where the middle 494 shots go to die.

By the time you're on your last three balls, though, you've finally given up on being perfect. You're too tired to experiment, so you just swing naturally, and—surprise, surprise—you start flushing it again. It's like the golf gods reward you for finally shutting up and just swinging.

I walked away from that day at Exec with two thoughts. First, Hal Underwood was operating on a higher plane of existence. Second, the Underwood Theory might just be the simplest, truest explanation for what goes wrong during practice. It's not about grinding until you're perfect; it's about not letting your brain get in the way.

The next time you're at the range, remember this: Hit your first three with confidence, accept that you're going to screw up the middle ones, and save your energy for a strong finish. If it worked for Hal Underwood, the best amateur in the country, it might just work for the rest of us.

John Mills's Winter Golf Theory: The "Play Short" Strategy

When it came to winter golf in Texas, on unforgiving courses with a strong north wind, my roommate John Mills was like a mad scientist with his own playbook. While the rest of us were busy trying to battle the elements head-on, John had a brilliant but very simple method. One that seemed counterintuitive at first but made a world of sense when you saw it in action. His approach? Play short on every hole. Hit purposely short. Leave yourself an uphill chip and play for par. It might sound way too safe, but when the wind is howling and the fairways are cold and rock-hard, it's nothing short of genius. (Note: Remember, back then, we were playing with a balata ball, wooden-headed drivers, and fairway woods.)

The essence of John's plan was this: On a windy, cold, and long golf course, aiming for the green like it was any other day was like trying to wrestle a grizzly bear. The greens were tough to hold, the winds knocked your ball off-target, and anything long or off-line left you an often impossible recovery shot. It left much tougher up-and-downs, with possible double-bogeys. But if you come up just short, the ball will always be in a spot where you can usually get it up and down for par. It's always setting you up with an uphill chip, rather than an impossible side-hill pitch shot or a nightmare bunker shot.

You're essentially vastly reducing risk. John figured that if he could chip and pitch at a high level, he should save par nearly every time. By laying up short of the green, you give yourself a predictable, short-game challenge rather than wrestling with inconsistent approaches that might leave you with much tougher shots and bogeys, or worse. And for those of us who played with him, his method led to a ton of stress-free pars.

Think about it: By playing short, you avoid the traps that lie in wait around most greens on tough courses: bunkers, thick rough, even water hazards. John's logic was that you're cutting out the worst-case scenarios. Sure, you're giving up a shot at most birdie opportunities, but John would also take advantage of shorter holes or front pin placements. He was effectively eliminating big numbers, especially on days when the wind was blowing so hard, it felt like the ball had a mind of its own.

Remember, on any course, there were a few scoring holes where John would aim at flagsticks.

John was very clever and also a realist. He knew that some holes were going to present real birdie opportunities, especially on par-5s or shorter par-4s. His strategy wasn't about turning down every birdie chance, but about knowing when to pick his battles. On a course with a few forgiving holes or reachable par-5s, he'd take his chances. For sure, he would hit some greens in regulation. But for the rest of the course, he kept his game in check.

By the end of the round, John's scorecard might not have a slew of birdies, but it'd be clean, consistent, and often with very few bogeys, especially when conditions were at their toughest. His strategy kept him in control, and it was a master class in knowing when to press forward and when to play it safe.

I'll never forget a round we played on Jackrabbit, one of the great courses at Champions Golf Club, on a cold winter day in Houston when scores soared. Mills pulled in with a 72 on a course we played from the tips at over 7,200 yards. He hit only four greens in regulation.

What did I learn from watching John play golf in the winter? Sometimes, the smartest path to a low score wasn't fighting the course, but working with it. John's strategy was about setting himself up for a manageable par on every hole, rather than letting ego or the occasional rush of ambition cloud his judgment. It was a simple plan, but it worked wonders.

I often think about how John Mills strolled around the golf course, with his unshakable strategy, making par after par on a brutal winter day, and that was a thing of beauty. Oh, and I might've left out one small detail: John was a great short putter, and being from Maine, tough as nails.

As John would remind us with a smirk, "It's easier to chip up to a hole than to pitch over a bunker." So next time you're facing a long shot to the green with a thirty-mile-per-hour, left-to-right wind, I suggest you think about the "Play Short" strategy. Leave yourself an uphill, short shot to the pin. You'll be smiling when you have a makeable putt instead of dreading a tough chip or pitch across a hard, fast green.

Muhammad Ali

In 1971, Muhammad Ali fought Buster Mathis in Houston. When I found out you could watch Muhammad train for two dollars, I knew immediately that I had to be there. It was my junior year at the University of Houston, and my roommate John Mills and I jumped at the chance to see the legend up close.

We arrived early, securing fantastic seats about five rows from the ring. When Muhammad walked into the gym, passing right by us, the sheer size of him was striking—about six feet, three inches and in incredible shape. I remember hearing boxing writers say Muhammad didn't hit as hard as some other top heavyweights, but once he started pounding the heavy bag, that notion quickly vanished. The power of his punches was astonishing: Each strike echoed through the gym like a thunderclap. The idea that he lacked power suddenly seemed absurd. It was clear this man was a force of nature.

Watching him train was mesmerizing. Muhammad started by jumping rope, moving with unbelievable speed and coordination. But what caught my attention even more was Bundini Brown. I'd seen him on TV alongside Angelo Dundee during fights. But in training, I saw the crucial role he played. Bundini never left Muhammad's side. He constantly chanted encouragement, shouting, "You were born to be the champion!" and the famous "Float like a butterfly, sting like a bee!" The intensity and sincerity of his encouragement made me realize something important: Even the greatest athletes need someone who continuously believes in them.

It brought my mind immediately to how Coach Williams often did the same. Coach was just like Bundini—always at our sides, always boosting our confidence. He never missed an opportunity to brag about us. He would tell anyone who'd listen that we were the greatest college golf team in the nation. Sometimes it was embarrassing. I remember cringing when he would openly boast about our accomplishments, often exaggerating them just a bit. At the time, we didn't understand what he was doing. We thought it was just his style, just part of his personality. But, looking back, I now see how incredibly powerful that constant positivity and encouragement was.

Coach's bragging wasn't just talk—it was strategy. He was building us up, constantly reinforcing our self-belief and convincing us we could achieve anything. And it worked. We began to believe in ourselves the way he believed in us, and that belief was a huge factor in building the Houston Dynasty. We didn't fully grasp it then, but Coach knew exactly what he was doing. He knew that champions weren't just made by skill alone, but by confidence, belief, and the unwavering support of someone who saw your greatness even before you saw it yourself.

That lesson from Muhammad's training and Coach's constant encouragement shaped the coach I later became. I carried that same approach into my own teaching, making sure my junior golfers always knew how great they were. I told them they could beat anyone, and many times, they did. I applied the same philosophy with tour players and amateurs, always striving to be that voice in their corner, pushing them to greatness.

The impact of watching Muhammad and understanding the importance of Bundini's role, combined with experiencing Coach's unwavering belief in us, stayed with me forever. It was a simple yet powerful lesson: Everyone, no matter how great, needs someone by their side to remind them just how extraordinary they truly are.

7

YOU HAD TO BE THERE

Setting the Temperature

When I roomed with Bruce Lietzke, Bill Rogers, and John Mills, we had a nice, little two-bedroom apartment. Bruce and I shared one room, and Bill and John bunked in the other. Bruce and I were temperature comrades. We liked it cold—the kind of cold that'd make a polar bear think twice. And we kept that bond strong. Not only did we room together on every away trip, but even on the mini-tours when we turned pro, we still shared a room and froze each other out, just the way we liked it.

Note: *In San Diego, when we played professional golf after college, Bruce and I played a ten-week mini-tour series. Some may not realize how cold it gets at night during the winter months near the Pacific Ocean, but that wasn't cold enough. We had a floor unit that would get our room so cold, you could see your breath. In that* *hotel room, we had big comforters that we pulled over our heads at night. Bruce kept a golf club next to his bed so that, in the morning, he could reach out and hit the heat button. Then, after fifteen minutes or so, we could get out of bed. I never slept better.*

Bill and John, on the other hand, had what I'd call an "opposite" relationship with room temperature. They liked it warm. No, not just warm. I'm talking sauna-level, thick-as-molasses air, at a stifling seventy-five degrees. They'd crank the thermostat up like they were trying to ripen tomatoes in our living room. Coming from the cool climate of the Northwest, I wasn't used to sleeping in temperatures that high. Back home, I'd never slept a single night above sixty-eight degrees. Heck, fifty-eight was my comfort zone. So, as you can imagine, this set us up for a bit of a thermostat tug-of-war.

Here's how it went: Whoever stayed up the latest got to set the thermostat to their liking. Bruce, bless his night-owl soul, was a man who liked to wind down slowly. He'd watch TV, read a magazine, or do whatever else he did before bed, just to make sure he was the last one awake. That meant, nine times out of ten, the place was set to "meat locker." If it got down to a brisk sixty-five degrees, Bruce and I slept like babies while Bill and John bundled up like they were camping in the Rockies.

And believe me, the sight of those two in the morning, buried under layers of blankets, was priceless. I once caught John with three pairs of socks on and a scarf around his neck, shivering like he'd been caught in an arctic blast. Meanwhile, Bruce and I were sprawled out, sleeping peacefully in a cool haven that would make a penguin feel right at home.

But on those rare occasions when Bill or John managed to stay up later than Bruce, the tables were turned, and the thermostat would sneakily creep up to seventy-five. I didn't have to see it to know—I could *feel* it. I'd wake up around 2 a.m., drenched in sweat, like I'd been running laps. The room would be thick and muggy, and I'd lie there, sticking to the sheets, wondering if I'd somehow been transported to the equator. I'd toss, I'd turn, and I'd try to sneak over to the thermostat to dial it down without getting caught.

It was an unspoken war, and nobody ever officially declared a winner. But Bruce, with his trusty late-night habits, held the advantage most nights. The way they saw it, that thermostat was a life-or-death situation, and Bill and John were not shy about voicing their misery. They'd grumble, "Dang, you two are gonna freeze us to death in here!" And we'd just shrug, content with our icy oasis.

I'd bet Bill and John slept under more blankets in a single semester than anyone in Houston, Texas.

The Ice Storm Incident: Albuquerque-Bound

It was the fall of my junior year, and we were heading out to Albuquerque, New Mexico, for the Tucker Invitational. This wasn't just any road trip. This was my first time experiencing the legendary *fourteen-hour marathon drive* from Houston to Albuquerque, with our amazing Coach Dave Williams leading the charge in his infamous green station wagon.

If you haven't heard about Coach's green station wagon, let me set the scene. It was an older, light green wagon disguised as a car. It did have power steering and a radio but certainly no seat belts. It was about as aerodynamic as a brick.

On this trip, I was riding with another one of my roommates, Bruce Ashworth. I was lucky to be in the second car with him. This would be his last Tucker, and he knew the ropes. Bruce could've made it to Albuquerque in about ten hours flat if he'd been allowed to drive the lead car. But no, Coach made it a rule that the second car had to follow him, which meant we were chained to the pace of the green machine.

We hit the road at the crack of dawn because, as Coach put it, "We ain't stopping till the Texas border, boys." But we did stop occasionally for burgers, and by "occasionally," I mean when Coach was low on coffee or we demanded a bathroom break.

Somewhere out in West Texas—so flat you can see the next town three counties over—a storm started brewing. Not just any storm though: a monster storm. The kind where you can see black clouds stretching to the horizon and sheets of rain falling hard. Only it wasn't raining; it was golf ball–sized hail.

Bruce and I were in the back car, watching this apocalyptic scene unfold, but up ahead, Coach was unfazed. It was only later when we learned that Corker DeLoach, in Coach's car, said, "Coach, this storm's looking bad. Maybe we oughta pull over."

But Coach, looking over at the fast-approaching, massive black cloud, had a different thought, and he was determined. He wasn't having it.

"Boys, we're not stopping. I'm gonna outrun this storm."

Outrun the storm? There are two things you don't do in West Texas: argue with the weather and try to outrun an ice storm. Coach, however, had a level of confidence that could've convinced you the laws of nature didn't apply to him.

The rain started first, coming down in sheets so thick it felt like we were driving through a car wash. Then the ice balls hit. Corker and Arthur Russell in the back seat were now getting ready to dive under their seats. Coach was white-knuckling the wheel, muttering under his breath about how "we can make it." Then came the ice. Then, *wham!* It was like somebody opened the freezer door and dumped out the ice maker.

We watched in horror as Coach's green machine started to shimmy, then slide, then spin like it was auditioning for *Dancing on Ice*. Before we knew it, the wagon did a full 360-degree spin and skidded off the road, coming to rest in a ditch.

Bruce and I were quite a ways behind as we had dramatically slowed down. We made our way, slowly, to the station wagon and came to a stop just in front of the ditch. The storm was now passing, but the road was a white sheet of ice.

There he was, Coach, still in his seat, gripping the steering wheel like he'd just executed a perfect landing. Corker was in the passenger seat, looking like he'd seen the afterlife.

Bruce and I came out of the car and asked, "Y'all okay?" Because, at this point, we thought someone might be hurt.

Coach turned to us, deadpan, and said, "Yeah, I was so close to beating that sucker." Bruce and I just looked at each other. What could you say?

We helped push the green machine out of the ditch and got back on the road, moving at Coach's normal pace, unfazed for the rest of the trip. Coach never mentioned the spinout again—because, in his mind, it never happened. To him, it was just another leg of the journey.

We eventually made it to Albuquerque, still laughing about Coach's attempt to "outrun" Mother Nature. It could have been a disaster. But, hey, that was life on a Dave Williams road trip. It wouldn't be until next year when we would finally fly to Albuquerque. I think Coach realized that it was time. He had made that drive, somehow safely, for eighteen years since 1953.

Missing the Flight to Albuquerque

It's one year later, and, for the first time ever, the University of Houston golf team is flying to Albuquerque for the Tucker Invitational, one of the biggest college tournaments of the year. Usually, in the hallowed tradition of Houston golf, we'd pile into Coach's infamous green station wagon and white-knuckle it through the fourteen-hour drive. I just told you about last year's ride—the frightening experience of Coach's haphazard driving. So you better believe we were thrilled to skip that highway to hell and hop on a plane this time.

Bruce Lietzke was our designated driver to the airport. Back then, security was nonexistent—nothing like today. You could slide in fifteen minutes before takeoff, flash a grin, and walk straight onto the plane. We were depending on this. We figured we had all the time in the world even though, truth be told, we were already cutting it very close. Bruce, Bill Rogers, John Mills, and I tossed our clubs and bags in the trunk and set off for Hobby Airport, definitely in no rush.

When we finally rolled up to the airport, we were moving at a speed that could only be described as "unhurried." We checked our bags with zero urgency and eventually made our way to the gate, still feeling unhurried.

There was Coach, standing at the gate, looking worried. He was tapping his fingers on the desk in front of the podium. Arthur Russell was sitting in a chair behind Coach, looking back at us and indicating with his hand that we should move it a bit faster.

Arthur had been sitting there, waiting two hours for us to get there. He wasn't about to be late for this flight—not with Coach always making him the scapegoat of any mishaps. As the fifth man on the team, this was also an extremely important tournament for him, with a chance to solidify a spot for the remainder of the year.

So there we are, finally hurrying a bit to arrive at the gate, when Coach confidently told the attendant, "Everyone's here!" like we've somehow arrived in the nick of time. The only problem? The plane was already rolling backward, slowly moving away from the gate. We'd missed it—no way around it.

Coach stared out at the plane, his jaw practically hitting the floor. He slammed six tickets down on the podium with all the authority of a Texas sheriff.

"Bring that flight back!" he ordered, like the attendant had a magic lasso to reel the plane back in. Everyone near us snapped their heads around to see what the heck was going on.

The gate attendant gave him a look and said, "Sir, it's too late. FAA rules. The plane is gone."

Coach absolutely couldn't believe they were not going to bring the plane back in for the Houston Cougars golf team. Once again, he told the attendant who we were. Obviously, they had to bring the plane back in for us. The attendant just shook his head, and that was it.

Coach looked like his world had just crumbled around him. He planned this whole trip to the second, and now his brain had short-circuited. He spun around, his face redder than a Lone Star sunset, and landed squarely on poor Arthur.

"Arthur!" he yelled. "I told you to be here on time! Now look what you did—we missed the flight!" Arthur took the blame!

And just like that, Coach declared that we were going to drive to Albuquerque. He wanted to load us all up in the station wagon for another fourteen-hour ride across Texas and New Mexico. It didn't matter that there was no way we'd get there in time for a practice round.

That was when John Mills, ever the voice of reason, quietly reminded Coach that, you know, we could just . . . take a later flight. It was like a lightbulb flickered over Coach's head—he hadn't even considered that option. His mind had been blown away by this plane leaving without us.

So, eventually, once he cooled down, that was what we did. We took a later flight, and everything was okay.

One thing was definitely true though: Coach sure as heck wasn't about to pin this on his top players. Oh, no, that wouldn't fly. If you were one of his stars—or "studs," as he liked to call us—you could get away with just about anything.

So, while Arthur took the full brunt of Coach's explosion, the rest of us just stood there, trying not to grin. We felt bad for Arthur, sure. But we were secretly both amazed and relieved that Coach Williams had exonerated the four of us. After all, we were the ones who were late; we were the sole reason for missing the flight. But Arthur, on the other hand, would be walking on eggshells on this trip, just as he had all year!

No Seat for You

Arthur Russell had already put himself in the doghouse before we even teed up at the Tucker Invitational. After we missed our flight to Albuquerque and had to wait about eight hours for the next one, Arthur had somehow taken the blame for all of it. He had been at the airport early for that flight while my teammates and I were the ones who were late. But, in Coach's eyes, if you were on the team and playing well, then you were not likely blamed for small mistakes. Sometimes even big ones.

Arthur, on the other hand, had qualified for the last spot. As a qualifier, there was no room for poor golf on this trip; he definitely needed to play well. We all expected that Arthur would because of his awesome ball-striking talent. He had worked hard and earned this trip, playing great golf, and, wow, the opportunity was there for Arthur to solidify a spot on the team.

It was one of the biggest college tournaments in America, and all eyes were on Houston as the defending champions. Yes, we had started this trip by missing the flight—which put Coach in a bad mood for sure—but the team played well, and after we won another Tucker and beat Texas once again, Coach's mood improved tremendously.

The only negative was Arthur did not play well. It was not that he just played poorly. No, sir. He played the kind of golf that made you start considering alternative career paths, or maybe even dropping out of college.

It wasn't just one bad round though. It was a *Texas-sized* disaster. If scorecards had mercy rules, Arthur would've been showered and back at the hotel by the twelfth hole after his last day. His final number was high, including two rounds in the 80s, which was not allowed at Houston.

We had a very simple system: If you shot a high number, like high 70s, you were in trouble. If you shot *Arthur Russell's* numbers, you were looking at a one-way ticket back to the qualifiers at best.

But I'm not talking about the *real* qualifiers. No, he would have to qualify in a lower group and play well just to *get into* the actual final qualifying rounds. It was like getting demoted from the major leagues down three levels in the minor leagues to B ball.

When we arrived at the Albuquerque airport to head home, Arthur already looked like a man walking to the gallows. He was quiet. Real quiet. The kind of quiet that comes from deep dread. When we finally boarded the plane, we saw that there were five open seats right up front—one for Coach and four for the players. But, of course, we had five players.

Coach looked around, did a quick head count, then locked eyes on Arthur like a judge about to hand down a death sentence.

"You go to the back of the plane."

Normally, a coach might cushion a blow like that. Maybe a "tough break, kid" or a "next time, you'll get 'em." Not Coach Williams. Not after a score like Arthur's. This was *banishment*.

Arthur blinked and looked around, waiting for someone—anyone—to step in. But he knew. We all knew. There wasn't a damn thing to say. So with the posture of a man who had lost everything in a bad poker hand, Arthur gathered his things and started the long, lonely walk down the aisle.

The rest of us settled into our premium, front-row seats. We stretched out, ordered our drinks, and enjoyed our victory ride back to Houston, knowing full well everyone back in the dorm rooms would be asking about Arthur's high rounds.

Arthur, meanwhile, found his assigned spot—the *very last seat* on the plane, right next to the toilet. That was, of course, the seat the airline only gave out when they absolutely had to. It was where the unlucky soul sat, where the bathroom door swung open every two minutes, and where you were in constant danger of getting smacked in the knee by a passing beverage cart. It was, without a doubt, the worst seat in the house.

And then, out of nowhere, a miracle.

Just as the plane was preparing for takeoff, a drop-dead gorgeous flight attendant made her way to the back of the plane. Wouldn't you know it, a jump seat *right next to Arthur*.

Keep in mind, Arthur was in no condition to be social. He looked like a man who had just been fired, dumped, and/or audited all in the same day. But, somehow, against all odds, they struck up a conversation.

And somehow she liked him.

We don't know what was said. Maybe she had a thing for sad, defeated men. Maybe she mistook his thousand-yard stare for mystery. Or maybe she just liked his Southern charm. Whatever it was, by the time we landed in Houston, Arthur had done what was impossible. He had not only gotten her number—he had set up a *date*.

It took forever before Arthur finally walked off the plane and caught up with us. But then, right there in front of the whole team, the flight attendant walked up to Arthur, smiled, and said, "I can't wait to see you in a few days."

I swear, you could *hear* our jaws hitting the floor. None of us could believe it.

Arthur Russell—who had played so badly, he was lucky Coach even let him *on* the plane—had just pulled off the greatest comeback we'd ever seen.

He wouldn't see another tournament round for a long, *long* time, but it didn't matter. Arthur had just won the most important match of the trip.

Sneaking Over the Border

Back in 1971, crossing the Rio Grande wasn't quite the international incident it could be today. Sure, it wasn't entirely safe, but it also wasn't like there was a cartel waiting for you at the edge of the water. Still, one thing was for sure: Our coach, the legendary Dave Williams, would have none of it. Crossing the border into Laredo, Mexico, was absolutely, unequivocally, 100 percent forbidden.

So, naturally, we did it anyway.

It all started when we rolled into Nuevo Laredo the night before the Border Olympics tournament. Coach Williams had us on a tight schedule: dinner at a local all-you-can-eat spot, followed by a team meeting from 8:30 to 9 p.m. Then it was supposed to be straight to our rooms to "get a good night's sleep" before the first round.

But let's be honest: What college golfers in Texas were going to spend the night before a tournament tucked into bed like choirboys? Especially when the lights of Laredo were practically calling our names?

Coach, of course, gave us his usual speech at the end of the meeting. You know, the one about the "dangers" of crossing the border. He went on about how "absolutely no one on this team better even think about it." He gave us the look—the one that could peel the paint off a golf cart—and sent us to our rooms.

As soon as we closed the door, the plan we had put together on the drive went into action. My roommate, as always on road trips, was Bruce Lietzke. He had driven his orange Dodge Charger—a 440-cubic-inch beast that growled louder than a Texas thunderstorm—all the way down to Nuevo Laredo. We just had to figure out how to sneak out without Coach hearing us.

Anyone who had ever met Coach knew he had the ears of a coyote. If Bruce so much as turned that Charger's ignition in the parking lot, we'd be dead men walking. So we did what any clever, slightly foolish college golfers would do: We pushed the car out of the lot.

Yes, you heard that right. Five college guys in jeans, shoving a bright orange Charger down the hotel parking lot like we were launching a rocket. We didn't start the engine until we were safely around the corner and out of Coach's earshot. Once Bruce fired it up, that beast roared to life, and we were off.

When we got to Laredo, we were the last team there. Turns out, most of the other teams had arrived hours before. It was like a reunion—college golfers from all over America, blowing off steam and pretending we didn't have a tournament the next morning. We hit the bars, shared some laughs, and told some fantastic stories.

By the time we rolled back into the hotel parking lot, it was close to 2 a.m. We pushed the Charger back into its spot (quietly, of course) and snuck into our rooms. As far as we knew, we'd gotten away with it.

The next morning, we showed up to the course ready to play. Nobody seemed worse for wear, and Coach didn't say a word. Not one. He just gave us that same knowing look he always did: the one that made you feel like he could read your mind. Did he know? Maybe yes? Maybe not? Coach had a way of knowing things he shouldn't. But he didn't say a word about it, and neither did we. No harm, no foul.

Looking back, it's one of those stories that only makes sense in Texas. You don't just sneak across the border in a car so loud, it could startle a herd of cattle, then push it around a parking lot to avoid getting caught and end up playing an eighteen-hole, top-college tournament the next day like nothing happened. But, hey, we were young, fearless, and definitely just a little bit dumb. And somehow, it all worked out.

Guadalajara, Gunfire, and Golf: A Texas-Style Tale

I've been in some wild situations in my life: college dorms full of rowdy golfers, bunkers that seemed deeper than my student loan debt, and Texas summers hot enough to cook a steak on a sidewalk. But nothing quite prepared me for what happened one night in Guadalajara.

Every once in a while, a Houston player would be invited to play in a professional event down in Mexico. I received such an invite in the fall of 1972. I was paired in the top threesome, playing alongside top European golfer Ramon Soto and a young Johnny Miller, who, as we all know, went on to win the 1973 US Open at Oakmont. That week, Johnny and I even did a clinic together before the tournament, and I developed a relationship with him where I could continually get his ideas on the game.

You'd think my biggest concern that week would have been how to keep up with Johnny's brilliant iron shots or low scoring. But no. The real hazard turned out to be an evening out in town.

After the practice round, a few of us competitors decided to embrace the local culture, which, of course, meant heading to a bar in Guadalajara for a casual beer. Nothing fancy, just a hole-in-the-wall joint that looked like it had seen its fair share of bad decisions. The kind of place where the bartender had a scar and the jukebox was stuck playing ranchera music at full blast.

We were minding our own business, sipping on cervezas, talking about how Mexican golf courses had more rocks than fairway grass, when out of nowhere—*BANG! BANG!*

Two gunshots.

I don't know what my reflexes were like on the golf course that week, but let me tell you: I dropped to the floor faster than a chili pepper in a bowl of queso. My playing partners weren't far behind. The whole place turned into the world's worst limbo contest, with everybody ducking, diving, and trying to make themselves as invisible as possible.

There's an old Texas saying: *If you hear gunfire and don't know what it's about, head the other way, pronto.* I didn't wait around to find out if someone had lost a poker hand, insulted the wrong señorita, or just didn't like the way his beer was poured. We left those beers on the table and got out of there so fast, I was halfway back to the hotel before I realized I still had my golf glove on.

The next morning, I had to shake off the excitement of my near brush with the Wild West (south-of-the-border edition) and get back to work as mentioned. I was playing the first two rounds with Johnny, who, despite his boyish looks, had a steely focus that made you think he'd been forged in some kind of golf laboratory. Johnny had exploded onto the national golf scene when he finished eighth at the US Open at age nineteen.

Johnny didn't know about my adventure the night before—or at least, I didn't bring it up. But if my hands were shaking a little on that first tee shot, it wasn't nerves from the competition. It was from realizing I nearly bought the farm the night before.

I managed to put together a respectable couple of rounds, but Johnny was in another stratosphere, grabbing the thirty-six-hole lead. A few months later, he went on to tear apart Oakmont and win the US Open with a legendary 63 in the final round. Meanwhile, I was just happy to be alive and still playing golf, knowing I had survived what might have been my closest call with disaster.

If I took away anything from that night in Guadalajara, it was this: Never leave a good beer behind—unless bullets are involved. Meanwhile, Johnny led the tournament after two rounds, but then left. I didn't quite get the story why. Who knows?

Golf is a game of survival—sometimes in the sand, sometimes in the rough, and, if you're lucky, only once in a while in a bar in Guadalajara.

8

STORIES I TELL AT THE NINETEENTH HOLE

The All-Night Party

It was a Friday night, and most of us had gone out for a team dinner. We were scheduled to play the next morning in one of those Houston Cougar/member events, a pro–am-type tournament we'd play at various clubs around the city. These events with the membership were great for letting us play on nearly any course in Houston. Coach made sure we all did a good job playing and socializing at every private club. Obviously, with forty guys on the team, we needed many courses to play, and it was really nice to be able to play the finest clubs in Houston.

But there was one small issue with these member events: early tee times. We're talking 8 a.m. on a Saturday morning, including the one-hour drive out to this course, which meant any Friday night fun was supposed to wrap up early. *Supposed to*. But this particular Friday, one of the guys (who shall remain nameless) had a bright idea. "Let's not sleep at all! We'll stay up all night and go straight to the course. See what happens!"

The more we thought about it, the more genius it seemed. We convinced ourselves it was a team experiment, a bonding exercise. Maybe we'd set a record for the best rounds on zero sleep. So we all agreed: no sleep, then head straight to the course and play eighteen holes with the members. A cool experiment. What could go wrong? Most of us hammered down a few beers as we laughed and told stories.

We all made it to about 4 a.m. before things started to unravel. Eyes were drooping, heads nodding, and bodies were slumping. But by sheer willpower, everyone stayed awake. Well, maybe a couple guys took an accidental nap for fifteen minutes, but we didn't hold it against them.

At 6:30 a.m., we caravaned to the golf course, which was a solid hour drive away, as a collection of zombie-eyed college golfers who looked like they'd barely survived a party. As we pulled into the parking lot, Coach was already there, looking sharp. Several guys could barely stand up straight, but Bruce Lietzke looked particularly rough. He'd driven out with Bill Rogers, and when Coach saw his young star player looking peaked, he walked over and asked, "Bruce, are you all right?"

Bruce, with bloodshot eyes barely open, mumbled, "Yeah, I think I'm all right, Coach."

Bruce was starting on the tenth, a short par-3 over a small pond. We were playing a shotgun start so everyone had a different hole. The tenth hole was only about 130 yards to the green, with a small pond that wasn't even in play. The pond required a ninety-yard carry from the back tee, where we were playing.

Bruce ambled over to the tee, pulled out his 9-iron, took a wobbly stance, and swung.

His divot was about three inches behind the golf ball, and his ball carried eighty yards straight into the middle of the pond. Coach happened to be watching the whole thing, horrified. He sprinted over to the tee, concern turning into disbelief, and practically yelled, "Bruce! Bruce! Bruce! What happened? My goodness gracious, you must be so sick! You need to go home! You're clearly not feeling well." He grabbed Bruce by the shoulder and gingerly led him back to the clubhouse.

"Coach," Bruce mumbled, "I feel very bad, but I don't have a car. I came with Bill."

Coach immediately found a golf cart and drove out to find Bill Rogers, who wasn't looking too good himself. He explained to Bill's group that there was an emergency, and Bill would have to drive his roommate back home, or even to the emergency room . . . and sent him off with Bruce.

Before we knew it, the two of them were in the parking lot, back in the car, and driving down the street adjacent to the golf course—waving like they'd just pulled off the greatest escape in history. As they drove past the golf course, Bruce and Bill grinned like two kids cutting class, thrilled to escape the carnage awaiting the rest of us.

As for the round itself—well, it was a tough day, to put it mildly. Most of the team was running on fumes and making terrible decisions and weak swings. Someone would line up a putt, only to blankly stare at the ball as if he'd forgotten how putting worked. By the back nine, some of us were sleepwalking, using our clubs more like canes than anything else.

Against all odds, I managed to hold it together, making putts from everywhere. As all golfers know, when you're sick, or when you sometimes give up, you hit some amazing shots and tend to putt better than ever. I shot a 72. On zero sleep, that felt pretty good. I was certain I'd shot the low round of the day by a ton. But wouldn't you know it? My roommate Bruce Ashworth sauntered in with a scorecard reading 69. It was another amazing performance by our first-team All-American, proving, once again, that Ashmo could shoot a good round in his sleep. He literally did it this time.

So there you have it. We tried the all-nighter experiment, and, while we survived, I wouldn't recommend it as a training method.

Choking

When golfers talk about choking, they're usually talking about the soul-crushing kind that happens on the golf course—yips on a short putt, a chunked chip under pressure, or a player who takes three extra waggles and then hits his drive right off a water hazard. But one night in Baldwin House, we witnessed a different kind of choking: one that involved shaving cream, sheer chaos, and a guy who looked like a beached whale gasping for air.

David Schuster was a big guy—big swing, big appetite, big personality. He was one of those dudes who made you feel like the room got smaller when he walked in. His roommate John Grace, or "Gracie," as we called him, was the opposite: wiry, short, quick, and clever enough to make Wile E. Coyote look slow. Gracie had a reputation for being as precise with his pranks as he was with his golf shots. The guy could hit a ball straighter than a plumb line. And his pranks? Well, they usually landed just as perfectly.

Baldwin House was a hotbed of pranks. You couldn't walk ten feet without fearing an ambush. Open your door? A bucket of water might drop on your head. Walk down the hall? Someone might tape you to the wall. But that night, Gracie decided to go old-school: the classic shaving-cream trick.

There were about a dozen of us crammed into David and Gracie's dorm room that evening, shooting the breeze and reliving the day's golf rounds. David, as usual, was holding court, leaning back in his chair with his mouth wide open, ready to deliver one of his Texas-sized opinions. That was when Gracie saw his chance. With all the stealthiness of a cowboy sneaking up on a stray calf, Gracie scooped a Texas-sized handful of shaving cream from a can and crept up behind David. Timing it perfectly, he waited until David turned to make his next grand declaration, then *bam!*—he slammed that mound of shaving cream square into David's face.

Normally, this kind of prank ended with a roar of laughter, some swearing, and the victim plotting their revenge. But this time? David had his mouth wide open, mid-sentence, and the shaving cream flew down his throat like a greased-up armadillo diving into a gopher hole.

At first, we thought it was hilarious. David's face was coated in shaving cream, making him look like a frothy Sasquatch. But then he froze. His eyes went wide, his face turned a shade of blue that was alarming, even under Baldwin House's dim fluorescent lighting, and he dropped to the floor, clutching his throat like a cowboy choking on a rib eye.

THE HOUSTON DYNASTY

Let me tell you, the mood in that room shifted faster than a Texas storm. One minute, we were howling with laughter, and the next, we were staring at David sprawled out on the floor, looking like a cross between a dying fish and a busted tube of toothpaste. Somebody yelled, "He's choking!" which, as you can imagine, didn't exactly calm the situation.

A few of us stood there, paralyzed, unsure if we were watching the funniest prank of the semester or the tragic demise of our buddy David. Others sprang into action with all the grace of a bull in a china shop. Somebody slapped him on the back, which did absolutely nothing except make him groan like a wounded bear. Another guy tried to tilt his head back, but all that did was make him look like he was gargling whipped cream.

Finally, one genius—probably the only adult in the room, mentally speaking—ran to get the dorm manager. Now, this guy was a grizzled Texan who looked like he could wrestle a longhorn for fun. He barreled into the room, took one look at David, and yelled, "Move aside!" like he was about to perform an exorcism. Without hesitation, the dorm manager jumped on David's chest with all the force of a linebacker tackling a quarterback. I didn't think Schuster's chest could cave in like that, but, sure enough, after two or three compressions, a geyser of shaving cream erupted from his mouth like Old Faithful.

David coughed, sputtered, and finally took a big gulp of air, his face still smeared with remnants of the cream. He looked like he'd just fought off a grizzly bear and barely lived to tell the tale. The room erupted in cheers and nervous laughter, with half of us patting David on the back and the other half apologizing for not doing more than screaming, "He's choking!"

For the next twenty-four hours, Baldwin House was uncharacteristically quiet. David avoided Gracie, Gracie avoided David, and everyone avoided shaving cream. But, like all things in Baldwin House, the incident soon became legend. By the end of the week, David was back to holding court, Gracie was planning his next prank, and the rest of us were dodging beer cans and buckets of water like usual.

But here's the thing: To this day, I can't look at a can of shaving cream without thinking of David, blue as the night sky, choking on what might've been the world's most absurd near-death experience. Houston pranks may have been dangerous, but, man, they sure were memorable.

Answering the Phone for Jastrow

Terry Jastrow was supposed to be a Houston golf legend in the making. After all, he'd won the Texas Junior Championship—a feat so big in our world that Coach Dave Williams probably had his recruitment letter stamped and sent before Terry even tapped in his final putt. The guy had all the makings of a golf stalwart for Houston: smooth swing, sharp mind, and movie-star looks. But fate had other plans!

It all unraveled one sunny day in a qualifying round, when Terry, looking calm and collected as ever, set up for what should've been a routine pitch shot. Problem was, his ball was sitting in a gnarly lie, into the grain—a shot that makes even the most confident golfer a bit queasy. Even tour pros occasionally miss this shot; it's extremely easy to chunk.

This shot can be cruel because of that Bermuda grain. It's like trying to butter toast with a rusty spoon. I think everyone reading this story has chunked a grainy pitch shot sometime in their life. But Terry was already having difficulty with chip shots and normal pitch shots. This was no secret to the team. So we can only imagine that Terry's heart was beating a little extra fast as he set up to hit this particular shot. I'm quite sure the thought of a chunk entered his visual field.

Then it happened. Terry didn't just chunk it. No, it was far worse. His divot started about four inches behind the ball, and, to everyone's horror, the divot—yes, the divot—turned over and landed directly on top of his golf ball, pinning it to the ground.

It was the kind of shot that didn't just rattle you. It humiliated you. The rest of his group stood there, jaws on the turf, as Terry stared at his divot, now smothered like a pancake. It was official: This was more than a bad shot—this was the kind of disaster that branded itself onto your soul. Like a ghost that rattled its chains in the attic, this chunk would haunt Terry every time he stood over a pitch shot until he just stopped playing. He went from a good player to a chunk machine. From that day on, Terry couldn't hit a pitch shot to save his life. It was over—done and dusted—and Terry knew it. Everyone knew it, and certainly Coach knew it. His career as a golfer was over.

The divot flopping over his ball was a shot that nobody at Houston would ever forget. By the time I arrived at Houston, Terry was a senior and still had a room in the dorm at Baldwin house. He was helping Coach market tournaments and with his recruiting. While the rest of us competed daily and lived two-by-two in the dorms, forty golfers deep in one hallway, Terry had conveniently relocated occasionally to an off-campus apartment with Hal Underwood, who was taking a fifth year to finish his degree. Hal had been the best player in the US and the "college player of the year," so Coach, of course, allowed him a little extra, and that meant a free room at Baldwin House, rooming with Terry whenever he decided to spend a night or two at the dorm. Technically, Terry still had a room at the end of the hall, but you'd rarely see him there unless he was picking something up, or just checking in to say hello to his friends.

The only evidence of Terry's existence in Baldwin House? The ringing of his phone in his dorm room.

Terry had instructed me to answer the phone if I heard it ringing, as my room was very close by. Every now and then, I'd walk past his room, hear the phone ringing off the hook, and answer it. "Hey, uh, is Terry there?" some sweet voice would purr on the other end, clearly a cheerleader, coed, or some local beauty queen. I'd scribble down the message—usually a name and a phone number—and pin it to his door, like a telegram.

Whenever we saw Terry away from the dorm, he was always with a drop-dead-gorgeous young lady. It never failed. Later, Terry would marry movie star Anne Archer, and he would end up running ABC Sports and appear in a few movies too. He had a fabulous personality, along with the good looks and the ambition to excel—one of the reasons he came to play at Houston for Coach Williams.

The Curious Case of Nick Faldo, the One-Semester Wonder

There are plenty of names that come up when you talk about the University of Houston Golf Dynasty—guys who tore up the college circuit, won national championships, and carried on the legacy of Coach Dave Williams with major titles and legendary careers.

But then there's Nick Faldo.

Yes, *that* Nick Faldo—the six-time major champion, eleven-time Ryder Cup player, and the guy who would become one of the greatest tacticians in the history of the game. But if you had asked any of his teammates in 1976, when he briefly joined the University of Houston golf team, whether they thought Nick would turn into a Hall of Famer, they would have laughed you off the golf course.

Because in the one semester he spent at Houston, Nick Faldo was not at all remarkable.

Nick came to Houston in the fall of 1976, part of a long line of talented international recruits. The University of Houston had become a hotbed for future stars from all over the world, and the idea of a tall, proper Englishman joining our Texas-strong program wasn't all that strange.

But unlike some of the international players who had made an instant impact, Nick did not make even a tiny dent. The guys who played with him at the time don't recall anything spectacular about his game. In fact, most of them barely remember him at all. If you weren't keeping a roster sheet, you might not have even noticed he was there.

Coach Williams, the master recruiter who always had his eye on the next big thing, didn't lose a wink of sleep when Nick packed his bags and left before even one semester. If anything, he probably saw it as a win: one less guy to manage and one more spot to fill with a player who had some game.

Nick's quick departure wasn't all that unusual. Back then, Houston was a revolving door for many players, including the few international players who made the long trip to Houston. Some stayed and thrived, but many others showed up, realized that college golf in the US wasn't for them, and headed for greener pastures—usually back home. Texas could be a shock to the system, especially if you weren't used to the weather, the relentless competition, and the unique blend of Texas hospitality and sarcasm that made up our team culture. Plus, it was, as most know, an entirely different style of the English language. I'm sure Nick must've felt shell-shocked.

For a guy like Nick, who was already incredibly methodical and had a specific vision for his career, college golf probably felt like an unnecessary detour. And if his game wasn't that strong at the time, he likely wasn't going to crack the lineup and prove otherwise. So he hit the road, leaving little more than a blank space in the history of the University of Houston golf team.

Here's where the story gets interesting. Most guys who flame out of a top college program don't go on to become all-time greats. Nick Faldo did.

After leaving Houston, he went back to Europe, put his head down, and started grinding. He built his game from the ground up, focusing on his technique, his swing mechanics, and his mental approach. He became a star on the European Tour, winning many events and earning his way onto five Ryder Cup teams. But he wasn't satisfied.

Then came the biggest turning point of all: his partnership with David Leadbetter.

Nick made the gutsy decision to completely rebuild his swing, an almost unheard-of move for someone at that level. He and David broke down every aspect of his motion and reconstructed it with surgical precision. It was a brutal process, costing him about two years of peak performance. But when he came out on the other side, he was a different player entirely.

By the late 1980s and early 1990s, Nick Faldo wasn't just a good player. He was a major-winning machine.

He won three Masters and three Open Championships, cementing himself as one of the greatest players of his generation. He dismantled Greg Norman at the 1996 Masters, played a starring role in more Ryder Cups, and became known for his almost robotic consistency under pressure.

This was the same guy who made zero impression at Houston. But if Coach Williams ever had a moment of reflection about letting a six-time major winner walk out of his program, he sure never showed it.

Coach wasn't the sentimental type. He believed in the guys who stayed, the guys who *wanted* to be part of the team. If you left, well, that was your decision, and he wasn't going to lose any sleep over it.

And let's be honest: Nick wasn't Nick Faldo yet. The version of him that Coach saw was just another young golfer trying to find his way. The guy he *became* was the product of years of relentless improvement, precise coaching, and a mental discipline that set him apart from almost everyone else.

Still, it's always fun to play the *what if* game. What if Faldo had stayed at Houston? What if he had stuck it out, developed under Coach Williams, and became a star at the college level? Would he have accelerated his success? Or would he have just been another guy on the team, lost in the shuffle of so many other elite players?

My guess? He had to leave.

Nick's game wasn't ready in 1976. He needed time, space, and total control over his development. The University of Houston golf machine was designed to churn out great college players, but it wasn't a place for long-term swing overhauls or meticulous rebuilds. Nick was a different kind of project. And, in the end, he got it right. Nick Faldo may not have left a mark on Houston golf history, but he certainly left a mark on the game.

For those who were around when he was at Houston, it's still a wild thing to think about. One of the best players of all time walked through the doors, stayed just long enough to realize it wasn't for him, and then disappeared, only to reemerge years later as one of the most dominant forces in golf.

Coach Williams? He probably never gave it a second thought. But for the rest of us, it's one of the great could-have-been stories in college golf.

And it just goes to show: You never really know who's going to end up wearing a green jacket someday.

The Three Amigos: Freddie, Jimmy, and Blaine

Some legends are born, others are made, and a rare few are forged in the dorm rooms of Taub Hall on the University of Houston campus. In 1977, after my time at Houston, three young men roomed together who would go on to leave an indelible mark on golf: Fred Couples, Jim Nantz, and Blaine McCallister. They weren't just roommates—they were dreamers and eventually known as the "Three Amigos" of golf.

Fred Couples: Mr. Smooth Operator
Let's start with Freddie. Before he became a Masters champion and the world's number one golfer, Fred Couples was just a Seattle kid with a silky-smooth swing and an even smoother personality. Back then, he wasn't "Boom Boom" yet—he was just *Freddie*. His swing was so fluid, it could've been bottled and sold as an anti-stress tonic.

Effort wasn't Freddie's thing—on or off the course. He strolled through life like he was walking on a cloud, which, let's be honest, was part of his charm. His idea of preparation for a tournament? Show up, grab a bucket of balls, and casually stripe 7-irons like he was playing a lazy Sunday round. But here's just a little inside information: At one point, Freddie did practice and hit thousands of golf balls at the Jefferson Park Golf Range, run by my friend Steve Cole. Freddie's job was to pick the range for Steve, but he was usually pounding free-range balls—the reason he was there. Freddie played almost every day at Jefferson and wore out golf gloves, which his parents didn't appreciate. He had a strict limit on his spending habits, so Freddie just stopped wearing a glove, and that lasted his whole career. No glove—just like Ben Hogan and Bill Rogers.

Freddie's laid-back attitude wasn't laziness though. It was confidence. It was something that Blaine and Jim had never encountered. Blaine would be grinding on his putting stroke, Jim would be practicing his golf swing and his sports commentary relentlessly, and Freddie, sitting back, would be tossing a ball up and down, saying, "Y'all are overthinking it. Just hit the shot."

Jim Nantz: The Voice of Golf (and Taub Hall)
Then there was Jim Nantz, the only one in the room who showed up at college knowing exactly what he wanted to do: become the voice of golf. While most UH golf team freshmen were trying to figure out their swings, Jim was preparing for a microphone that would someday become an extension of his hand.

Jim's routine was, I'm pretty sure, unique. Late at night, after classes and practice, Jim and Freddie would stage mock Masters broadcasts. Freddie, of course, always played himself: "Fred Couples, the smooth-swinging Houston Cougar, lines up his putt for the green jacket." Meanwhile, Jim would provide the play-by-play, using his best Augusta-inspired baritone: "Hello, friends . . . It's a perfect day here at Augusta National, and Fred Couples is about to fulfill his destiny."

The thing is, they weren't just playing around. This wasn't college hijinks but rather manifestation. Freddie really did win the Masters, and Jim really did sit in the broadcast tower and call it. Years later, when Jim's voice echoed across Augusta as Freddie slipped on the green jacket, it was like a flashback to their late nights at Taub Hall. Jim Nantz is arguably the greatest sports announcer of all time, and not only for golf—final four NCAA basketball, CBS football, Super Bowls, and much more. Jim is well-known worldwide and one of the nicest human beings on the planet.

Blaine McCallister: The Texan Tinkerer
And then there was Blaine McCallister, the quintessential Texan. Blaine had that down-home charm and enough quirks to fill a Texas-sized golf bag. For one, he hit the ball right-handed but putted left-handed. Why? Because it worked. Blaine wasn't interested in convention; he was interested in results.

Blaine's explanation for his putting stroke was classic Texas humor: "If you're choking on a four-footer, switch sides. It confuses your brain long enough to forget you're nervous." And wouldn't you know it, Blaine's unconventional style earned him five PGA Tour wins and the utmost respect of his peers.

But Blaine was more than about technique. He was about grit. He could grind through tough rounds like a rancher mending fences in the scorching Texas sun. He had that "never back down" attitude that made him a constant contender and the guy you always wanted in your corner.

The real magic of the Three Amigos was their bond. They pushed each other, laughed at each other, and believed in each other's wildest dreams. When Freddie hit a pure shot on the range, Blaine would say, "Looks good, but let's see it when the wind's blowing forty miles an hour." When Jim practiced his Masters commentary, Freddie would chime in, "This all seems good with me."

These were more brothers than teammates. They shared everything—except, perhaps, Blaine's barbecue sauce recipes, which he guarded like a family heirloom.

Their time at Houston was about building new dreams, as Freddie went on to become one of the smoothest and most popular players in golf history; Blaine carved out his own legacy with grit, charm, and an unforgettable putting stroke; and Jim became the voice of CBS sports broadcasting, including delivering some of the most iconic calls in golf history.

But their story is more than about individual achievements. It's about how three young men, in a dorm room at Taub Hall, imagined a future that seemed far-fetched at the time—and then made it a reality.

In 1992, when Jim Nantz stood at Augusta National and called Freddie's win at the Masters, it wasn't just a milestone for Freddie. It was a victory for all three of them, and a reminder of late nights in Houston, big dreams, and the magic of friendship.

The Three Amigos redefined what it meant to dream big, work hard, and never forget where you came from. They even ran a huge charity event, entitled "The Three Amigos." And that, friends, is how legends are made.

Eviction

In 1972, my senior year, we won the All-American Championship. It was one of those moments you could just feel was going to stick with you forever. I had the luck (or maybe the challenge) of playing two rounds with Andy Bean and two rounds with Andy North, both from the University of Florida. Andy North would later win two US Opens while Andy Bean won ten PGA Tour events. They were really good—Florida finished second, with Texas coming in third. But our team? We were solid all the way through.

Back then, we had five players for each tournament like they do today, but with a big difference: Over the three or four rounds, the four lowest overall scores counted, not the four best scores each day as they do in the current NCAA golf model. That meant if you played really well for the first few days and fell apart the last day, your total score might not end up counting for the team. So if you were playing well for the first two rounds, you had to keep playing well for your total score to count over the three rounds. This brought upon a lot more pressure than what they expect today, where just the best four scores are taken each day and the worst score is kicked out. For us, every stroke counted, and every player had to battle to the very end. The team was depending on you. But we pulled it off.

Of course, after a win like that, a celebration was inevitable. Somehow, our apartment became the "official" party zone for the night. Before long, we had half the team, and a few folks I'd never seen before, crammed into our place, music blaring and spirits running as high as the Texas sky. It was a party to remember—or to try to remember anyway.

The whole apartment was packed, and things were getting loud. Somewhere in the middle of this deal, we had a guest appearance by the UT duo of Tom Kite and Ben Crenshaw, who were also our good friends. They weren't about to miss out on the fun, and their presence seemed to crank up the excitement even more. What started as a team celebration turned into a full-blown, no-holds-barred college party—the kind where you just knew things were going to get interesting.

As the night wore on, things started spilling outside into the apartment complex. You know how it goes: guys getting rowdy, laughing and hollering like we were out in the middle of a Texas pasture instead of a residential complex. But then, as if the party gods decided we'd had too much fun, things took a turn. One of the freshmen—feeling all too bold and clearly lacking judgment—decided he couldn't wait to find a bathroom and took a leak right on the window of the apartment next door. This wouldn't have been quite so bad if the shades weren't wide open and, even worse, if there hadn't been a husband and wife sitting there, catching the whole performance up close and personal.

In no time, someone called the cops. Suddenly, we saw the red-and-blue lights flashing outside, and reality hit like a cold slap to the face. Just like that, our championship celebration took a nosedive. We tried to keep things under control, but by the time the cops showed up, it was clear we weren't going to just get a warning and go back to business as usual.

Long story short, the whole thing ended with us getting evicted. We'd taken home the All-American Championship and, just as quickly, lost our apartment. I found myself scrambling to find a place to stay for the last two weeks of school, feeling like the Texas heat was bearing down harder than ever.

It wasn't exactly the victory lap I'd planned, but, looking back, it was pure college: a mix of triumph, chaos, and a lesson or two thrown in for good measure. The All-American win? That's a memory I'll always be proud of. The eviction? Well, let's just call that a reminder that some wins come with a price.

9

A HUMBLING GAME

Low Scoring Average: Lessons in Life

In my junior year in 1971, I was riding high. I'd won three college tournaments, including the LSU Invitational, which was my biggest college win of the season, against a stellar field with schools from all over the country. Back then, we also played quite a few tournaments close to home, mostly within one hundred miles of Houston. In those smaller events, Coach Williams would often enter two teams, because, well, we had the depth for it. The competition wasn't just with other schools but also with our own teammates. And trust me, beating those guys was no small feat.

But LSU? That was one of the bigger tournaments of the year. That was where you faced a very strong field, not just the guys on your team, and winning it put me squarely on the radar as one of the top players that year.

The only problem? Houston golf in 1971 wasn't just a team but rather a *herd* of thoroughbreds. We had eight or nine guys who could win any tournament in any given week. And most of them did. I might have had the lowest scoring average on the team and three wins under my belt, but that didn't mean I was a shoo-in for the upcoming NCAA Championship.

Here's who I was up against:

- Tom Jenkins: Steady as a Texas oak and a future PGA Tour winner. Calm and tough.
- Bruce Lietzke: Could hit a fade in his sleep and make it look like poetry in motion. Would go on to become one of the best ball-strikers on the PGA Tour, and a fourteen-time winner.
- John Mills: The man had finished second at the NCAA Championship the year before and was already a First-Team All-American.
- Corker DeLoach: A phenomenal competitor and overall athlete. A short-game wizard who could get up and down out of a cactus patch.
- Arthur Russell: Solid player. Top ball-striker
- Bill Rogers: The future Open Champion who had nerves of steel, even back then. Would later become the number-one-ranked player in the world.
- David Schuster: Another guy who was always on the hunt, never giving you an inch. A huge man who smoked the driver.
- John Grace: Always lurking. Super-straight ball-striker. A future Walker Cup member.

A HUMBLING GAME

By the time the season ended, every single one of these guys had either won a tournament or finished second. It was like the Wild West: Every event was a shoot-out, and they were all quick on the draw.

After the season wrapped up, I went back home to Seattle, feeling very confident I would be heading to the NCAA. I mean, how could I not be? Three wins, low scoring average, played in every tournament all year—it wasn't even a question in my mind that I'd be headed to the NCAA Championship. I just waited for the call to pack and leave.

Then the phone rang. It was Coach.

If you've ever heard Coach Williams deliver bad news, you know he could do it with the same nonchalance as a Texas rancher telling you the barn just burned down.

"Jim, I've made my decision for the NCAA team," he said, his voice calm as ever. "I'm taking Tom Jenkins and Bruce Lietzke. John Mills, of course, is going—he's a first team All-American. And I'm taking Bill Rogers and Corker DeLoach. That's the five."

There was a pause. I waited for my name. Surely, he hadn't finished the list. But he had.

It felt like someone had just hit me in the gut with a 1-iron. I couldn't believe it. I'd played in *every* tournament that year. I'd won three times. I'd been the most consistent player on the team. And, somehow, I wasn't going.

"Coach, I don't understand," I managed to say.

"Well, Jim," he replied, "you had a great year, but this is the lineup I think gives us the best chance."

And that was it. No sugarcoating, no room for debate. Coach had made his call, and I was out.

THE HOUSTON DYNASTY

Houston went on to finish second at the NCAA Championship that year, losing to the University of Texas. Let me tell you, second place at Houston wasn't something you celebrated. Second place was like showing up to a Texas barbecue and finding out they'd run out of brisket. It just didn't sit right.

Did I think they would've won if I'd been there? It kept me up at night, and I wasn't the only one who thought so either. I heard several around the program whisper that Coach might've overthought this one. But I know the guys that went to this NCAA were all tremendous players, all of them deserving, and all of us wanted to be on that team. Someone had to be left out.

That disappointment lit a fire under me for the rest of 1971. I was determined to prove that Coach had made the wrong call. If you've ever been left off a team you thought you deserved to be on, you know the feeling.

That summer, I qualified and played in the US Open at Merion. I won the Pacific Northwest Amateur for the second time, I won the Pacific Coast Amateur in San Francisco, I won the Seattle Amateur, I finished fourth in the US Amateur in Wilmington (that got me an invitation to the Masters), and I almost won the Northwest Open for the second year in a row. I had been the low qualifier for both the US Amateur and the US Open, and I was the sixth-ranked amateur in America. Maybe being left off that NCAA team had a lot to do with this great summer of golf.

In the end, though, that was Houston Dynasty golf for you. No matter how good you were, there was always someone just as good, or better, waiting in the wings. It was the ultimate college proving ground, and the pressure wasn't just a byproduct. It was the point. And if you couldn't handle disappointment, you'd better find another line of work.

Blair Douglass Goes Lights Out
(In More Ways Than One)

Blair Douglass showed up at the University of Houston with the kind of quiet presence that made you think, *Alright, let's see what this kid's got.* He wasn't a big name coming in but definitely another promising freshman. We quickly noticed a few things: Blair had a silky-smooth swing and power. His ball went sailing like it was trying to leave the state. It didn't take long for him to show us what he was capable of.

One week, early in the fall, he just caught fire. I'm talking ten rounds in the 60s in our qualifying—ten! The first five rounds didn't even put him in the top qualifiers, so no one really noticed. But he kept going, and he moved up to the first-tier qualifying group, and, wouldn't you know it, he fired off five more rounds in the 60s, with one "slip-up" at 70. That was all Coach needed to see to think he had another gem, another "stud" on his hands. Coach was probably up at night, dreaming of Blair becoming the next John Mahaffey, Fuzzy Zoeller, Bruce Lietzke, or Bill Rogers.

It was time to see what Blair could do in the real deal, as freshmen were now eligible to play varsity sports. Coach put him on the first team, ready to throw him against the best: Oklahoma State, Texas, SMU, Texas A&M, LSU, you name it. Coach was rubbing his hands together, thinking he'd struck gold with Blair.

I'd love to tell you that this story has a fairy-tale ending, but, well . . . this is golf, and, sometimes, it has a way of humbling even the hottest player faster than a Texas summer storm.

Coach decided to come out to the first tee and watch Blair tee off in his first varsity event, just to give him a little confidence. A nice thought, but apparently, and understandably, it exponentially increased Blair's nerves. He stood over that first shot, waggling the club, taking his time, swung, and knife-hooked the ball so far left, it was like it was trying to join the witness protection program. That ball shot off into the woods and was gone in a flash, like a space shot that veered immediately off-line.

And it went downhill from there. Blair tried to pitch out, but he hit a tree branch, the ball bounding straight down. From there, he chipped out again and ended up making a quick double bogey. By the time we got through the front nine, Blair had limped in with a 45. You could see Coach's dreams shattering, piece by piece, with every missed fairway and chunked chip.

Blair did a little better on the back nine, and the second round was . . . "poor," if we're being generous. But the damage was done. He finished far back in the pack, and Coach didn't need to think twice. Blair had his shot, and let's just say he didn't exactly light up the leaderboard.

And that was it. One shining amazing stretch of super-low rounds in the 60s, then a front-nine 45, and Blair was back to the bench. He never got another crack at the first team. His name may have faded quickly, but those of us who were there still remember it. For a few brief weeks, Blair Douglass had all the makings of a Cougar golf legend . . . until the legend went out like a candle in the wind.

A HUMBLING GAME

John Grace Is Not Going

Of all the incredible qualifying stories I ever heard, John Grace's journey is easily in my top five. This tale has everything you'd expect from the University of Houston: over-the-top competition, a super stubborn coach, and an underdog player who just got shafted.

We'd just wrapped up a grueling, eight-round qualifier to decide who would get the last spot on the team for the Border Olympics. Coach was determined to beat Texas this year. Sure, we'd been holding our own against UT, even winning most of the tournaments where both teams played, but with Ben Crenshaw and Tom Kite in the lineup, Texas was going to be extremely tough—especially in Laredo, where they played like they were born on those fairways.

Back to John Grace, who was a smaller guy with a very solid classic swing. He hit the ball pure, but, so far, he'd never managed to crack the starting five at Houston. He was a senior now, and if there was ever a time to make it, this seemed like it. And make it he did. Gracie played the best golf of his life, shooting rounds in the mid-60s like a machine. By the end of this qualifying, he not only won the qualifier, he destroyed it, finishing 26 under par and beating the next-best score by a full twelve shots. Twelve! I don't think Coach had ever seen that coming. It was a nightmare for him.

Here's the twist: Coach didn't like surprises. Gracie winning by a landslide? That was definitely a massive surprise. This wasn't going to stand because Coach kept thinking of one hole at Laredo where Gracie might not be able to carry the lake, visualizing Gracie hitting tee shot after tee shot into the water. So

Coach, in his infinite wisdom, decided the eight-round qualifier was just a "warm-up" for a brand-new, one-round showdown among the top three finishers. All starting even? This was the kind of move we'd seen from him before, but not when someone had just set the course on fire the way Gracie did.

Well, you can imagine how that went over with Gracie. I swear, the poor guy must've nearly had a heart attack. But, true to form, he shrugged it off. If he had to win another qualifier, so be it. And he almost did. He lost in a one-hole playoff. But the truth is, even if Gracie had won that qualifier, Coach would've likely kept tacking on extra qualifiers until Gracie finally didn't.

You see, Coach had this very scary recurring thought about Laredo. He knew the wind could whip up something fierce, especially on the sixth hole—a long carry over water. Coach figured that, if a thirty-mile-per-hour headwind was blowing, Gracie would never be able to clear the hazard. And if you couldn't clear that water, you'd be stuck on that tee, sending ball after ball into the drink until you ran out. Tournament over! Coach didn't want to risk that incredibly unlikely scenario.

We all thought this was a little, well ... crazy. What were the odds of a perfect, thirty-mile-per-hour wind hitting us dead on, at that exact hole? But that was Coach's reasoning. In his mind, this would probably happen if he let Gracie go.

We crunched some numbers, and, sure enough, it would take a 220-yard carry, under normal circumstances, to beat the lake. Into a gale-force headwind, however, it was probably 240 to 250 yards. But, of course, this was a hypothetical. Only you never know, Coach figured.

In the end, John Grace didn't go to Laredo. It had to be a crushing blow, but Gracie took it like a pro. He never complained

A HUMBLING GAME

or made excuses. He just sucked it up, got back to practice, and kept trying to make the team. The man was unbreakable.

And here's the best part: After college, Gracie went on to become one of the top amateurs in the US, eventually making the Walker Cup team—that was the top ten amateurs in the country, mind you. He was runner-up in the US Amateur, too, and played in two Masters.

This story illustrates the level of competition at the University of Houston. It took more than talent to survive. It also took grit. And John Grace had it in spades.

Street Shoes and Texas-Sized Ego

Brady Miller from Orange, Texas, strutted onto campus like he owned the place. He'd been a junior golf sensation back home, with enough trophies to fill a small Texas museum, and he wore his cockiness like a badge of honor. But the University of Houston golf team was a different beast entirely, not some high school rodeo. Brady was up against seasoned, top-ranked college players; the kind who'd as soon break his spirit as they would shake his hand.

Brady had this oddball habit of playing in street shoes. Yep, no spikes, no cleats, just plain ol' street shoes like he was going out for a jog instead of a round of golf. Coach wasn't thrilled, to say the least.

Coach was on him constantly. "Brady, you need proper golf shoes out there, son!"

But Brady just grinned that wide, Texas grin and told him, "Coach, I've got this. I play great in street shoes."

Well, as it turns out, he didn't play quite so "great" his freshman year. Sure, he made it into a few of the top qualifiers, but he was not the star he imagined himself to be. At least not yet.

One warm spring day out at Atascocita, a few of us were teeing it up for another round of qualifying. Brady had been catching grief all year from the upperclassmen about his oddball ways, and his choice of footwear was target number one. But Brady was as stubborn as a mule in the summer heat—there was no talking sense into him. We rolled up around 1 p.m., right on schedule. As always, no practice balls, just a couple practice swings, and we went straight to the tips on the first hole. That would be our visual "two steps from the tips" every day.

Everyone teed off, saving Brady for last. Maybe he was feeling the pressure, maybe it was his nerves, or, for certain, it was those street shoes, but when he swung, his back foot shot out like a dog on a freshly waxed floor. His whole body twisted, and his swing went so far off-course, it was like he was aiming at the wrong fairway. All he managed to do on his swing was just barely nick the ball with the heel of his driver.

And I mean *barely*. The ball made this sad little scoot directly sideways, rolling directly between his feet. You'd think that'd be bad enough—a mighty swing with nothing to show for it. But no, things went from bad to worse. The ball, almost like it was mocking him, kept rolling until it came to a slow, miserable stop right up against a tree trunk. Yes, Brad's ball locked against this tree. The ball had not gone forward, but it had enough speed to go between his feet laterally, not forward.

So here's Brady, one shot down, practically still standing on the tee box, staring at his ball nestled up to that tree. He takes the one-shot penalty drop, finally gets his two club lengths to drop, and guess where he ends up? Right back where he started, except this time, he's got no tee. He has to pull out his 3-wood just to get a shot off.

It was, hands down, one of the most embarrassing shots I've ever seen. In fact, it's right up there in the annals of Houston Cougar golf. Brady didn't say much after that. He just kept his head down, but the look on his face said it all: Maybe, just maybe, Coach had a point about those golf shoes.

And that's the thing about golf: It doesn't care how many trophies you've got or how much swagger you walk in with. The game will humble you faster than a summer storm rolling across the plains.

Throwing Away the Tucker, and Something Far More Important

It was my senior year, and we were back in Albuquerque for the Tucker Invitational. This tournament was notorious for testing your patience, your golf skills, and your ability to survive Mother Nature's worst. The year before, we'd played in weather so bad, it made West Texas windstorms look like a light breeze. Freezing cold, sideways sleet, and a wind that felt like it was trying to slap the taste out of your mouth.

That year, I managed a first-round 76, which was more than a good score. It was a miracle. I rank it as one of the very best rounds I ever shot in college. Most guys were handing in cards with scores in the mid-80s, and some in the 90s. There were only two other scores under 80. I promise you that we all felt like we'd been in a brutal prize fight. The looks on many faces were stunned and like they'd just gone through Navy SEAL boot camp.

But this year was different. The weather was more merciful—by Albuquerque standards—and I was playing the best golf of my life. By the time I got to the final two holes, I was *leading* the tournament. At least I felt sure I was leading. I just needed a decent finish. I'd even let myself imagine hoisting the trophy.

Then came the seventh hole. The fifty-third hole of this tournament.

Let me paint the picture for you: The seventeenth at the University of New Mexico Golf Course was a mean, nasty par-3—one you could probably imagine. It was uphill, 235 yards, and playing directly into a strong wind. Calling it a par-3 was generous; it was more like a par-4 in disguise with an attitude problem.

I pulled out my driver—because, really, what else do you do when you're staring up a hole designed to be brutal, even in good conditions? Sure, it was a tough hole, but I ended up butchering the hole badly and made a fat triple bogey. A very ugly triple bogey. My lead? Gone faster than free brisket at a Texas barbecue.

I also missed on the eighteenth hole—a par-5. I walked off with a par, handed in my card, and sat down, convinced I'd just thrown away the tournament.

But, as luck sometimes shines on you, I wasn't out of it yet. When the scores came in, I was tied for first. Not alone, mind you, but with three other guys, including my roommate that week, Bruce Lietzke.

Also in the playoff were Ray Leach, one of the most talented junior and amateur golfers I'd ever played with, and Dennis

Walters, a name that would later mean so much more to golf and to life.

Dennis was a phenomenal golfer, no question. Dennis played for North Texas State, who we competed against often. We also played together in the summertime amateur events, so he was a good friend. He could hit the ball as well as anyone and had the kind of talent that made you think he was destined for the PGA Tour. But, right after college, tragedy struck. A freak golf cart accident back in his home state of New Jersey left Dennis paralyzed from the waist down. Most people would've given up, but not Dennis.

After some extremely difficult dark times, he reinvented himself, teaching his upper body to play from a specially designed golf cart with a swiveling chair. He didn't just return to golf. He became an entertainer, an ambassador, and an inspiration. Dennis built a career out of showing people that obstacles don't define you. His dog, a key part of his traveling show, fetched golf balls and melted hearts as Dennis brought joy to thousands, especially junior golfers. If anyone ever embodied resilience and determination, it was Dennis Walters. Over the years, Dennis has won awards for his courage and was enshrined in the PGA Hall of Fame. Recently, he won the US Open for disabled golfers. He even shot a round of 74, breaking his age.

As for the playoff, well, on the first hole, Bruce "Leaky" Lietzke decided to end it quickly. Calm, cool, and with that lazy confidence he always had, he rolled in a short birdie putt and walked away with the individual win.

And me? Well, I never let Bruce forget the tournament I gave him. Handed it to him on a silver platter. I *gifted* Leaky that trophy with my triple bogey at the end of that tournament. Bruce, of course, loved it. He used to say, "You really didn't want to win that tournament anyway, and thanks, Mac."

Well, somebody had to win it, and in the end, I was happy my teammate got the victory.

The silver lining? The University of Houston won easily that week. We dominated the field and cruised to another win, setting ourselves up for what we thought would be yet another national championship.

But when I think back to that tournament, it's not just the triple bogey or Bruce's win that stands out. It's the realization that golf is as much about grace as it is about grit. Watching Dennis Walters go on to inspire the world reminded me that, even when the bogey train derails you, or worse, a triple bogey—or when life throws you off the cart—you can still find a way to turn it into something remarkable.

Some lessons, like that triple bogey, sting. Others, like Dennis's story, stick with you forever.

The 1972 NCAA Championship

Cape Coral, Florida, May 1972. The weather was hotter and more humid than you could imagine. And the wind was howling like a coyote on a moonlit night. The conditions would be extremely challenging on a tough golf course.

The stage was set for one of the most competitive NCAA Championships in history. The University of Houston was slightly favored and would definitely be in the thick of it, as usual. But our nemesis, the University of Texas, was gunning for us with their dynamic duo: Tom Kite and Ben Crenshaw. These two were the best in America: Ben sank more long putts than anyone in the history of golf and made ten footers in his sleep, and Tom played like he had laser guidance on every shot and was the best inside-ten-foot putter on the planet. Both of them could take it deep at any moment, raining down birdies in big chunks. If that weren't enough, the University of Florida rolled in with a stacked lineup that included Andy North, who'd go on to win the US Open twice, plus future tour stars Gary Koch and Andy Bean. Then add in Oklahoma State, Arizona State, and Wake Forest, featuring Jim Simons and Lanny Wadkins, all with stellar teams.

This tournament wasn't going to be easy in any way. It was going to be a street fight in gale-force winds, with a constant barrage of beach sand flying in your face. But, hey, we were the Cougars. We thrived on tough conditions, and Coach wouldn't have it any other way.

The trip started, as always, with Coach telling everyone we saw that we were the Houston Cougars. This could happen anywhere: as we walked down the street, or when we entered a grocery store. Coach might blurt out "Cougars" at any time, which embarrassed us terribly. One night, Coach got lost, as usual, driving to a restaurant. So as only Coach would do, he slowed to a dead stop as we drove past a man sprawled out on the sidewalk, clutching a bottle of whiskey. Coach, with all the seriousness of a man asking for directions to the nearest church, told John Mills to roll down the window and ask the guy for directions to the restaurant. John just shook his head, not even considering this directive for one second. He looked at Coach and very clearly said, "No." Coach huffed and muttered something about missed opportunities. Eventually, after five or six turns and one U-turn, we arrived at the restaurant. No worries.

The first round was as brutal as expected: thirty-mile-per-hour winds whipping sand from the nearby beach and out of the numerous bunkers. As always, I was wearing my contacts, and I was definitely aware that sand was ripping into my face and, of course, into my eyes. I was playing well, though, and carded a 70, putting me in third place, alone behind—you guessed it—Ben Crenshaw and Tom Kite, who both shot 4-under-par 68s. My teammates were solid, too, and we ended the day tied for the lead with Texas.

But the sand had done a major job on me. By the time I finished my first round, my eyes felt like they'd been sandblasted. They were as red as ripe Washington apples and blinking faster than a hummingbird's wings. Coach took one look and immediately realized this could be a major problem. Never one to waste time, he rushed me to an eye doctor. Diagnosis: scratched corneas. Prognosis: no contacts for two days. Solution: play in glasses.

I had brought my pair of glasses that I used to read at night or just to rest my eyes, but I never played golf in my glasses. I had never played any sport in my glasses—football, basketball, or baseball. I had been wearing contacts since age thirteen.

Let me tell you something about playing golf in glasses (although I'm sure most everyone knows): There's a drastic difference in the visual depth perception between contacts and glasses. When I put them on, my ball looked like a marble sitting on the horizon. But there wasn't a choice—I had to play.

A HUMBLING GAME

The second round was pure survival for me. My vision was shot, and I was swinging on pure instinct. I somehow limped through the first eight holes at +1, but then came the ninth—a par-5 with a lake guarding the green. I laid up to about 110 yards, but close to the lake. When I got to my ball, I saw Coach and Bill Rogers watching like hawks, obviously hoping I was hanging tough. I flashed to them that I wasn't bad at all.

When I got to my ball, I immediately saw that the lie was awful. My ball was sitting low in the rough, and, through my glasses, it looked like it was hiding in a gopher hole. I tried to block out Coach and swung. It was a semi-chunk, yet I thought it still had a slim chance of clearing, but no—*splash*. Into the lake. I'm now laying 5, and I've got the same shot to play again.

I had to drop another ball. In those days, you dropped it over your shoulder, which made it about as precise as throwing darts blindfolded. With the ball in my right hand, I dropped it over my right shoulder. To my horror, the ball bounced sideways into a crater-sized divot. Perfect. Now what was I going to do? I could chip out sideways, back to the fairway, or try to hit the shot over the lake again. Coach had now turned his back, waiting for Bill to let him know what happened. Of course, I tried to hit the shot over the lake to save a respectable score. But no, another chunk—a serious chunk—flies only halfway across the lake—*splash* again!

At that point, Coach couldn't take it anymore. He started walking and wandered off into the woods like a man who'd just seen his dog run away. I knew what he was thinking: *This kid's about to make a 15, and we're cooked.*

I didn't make a 15—I made a 9, which was about as bad. I shot 79 that day and followed it up with a 78 in the third round.

THE HOUSTON DYNASTY

Coach was in disbelief. On the final day, the eye doctor gave me the green light to wear my contacts again. I shot a solid 72, but it was too little, too late. Houston was about to finish in second place.

When I finished my round, I walked out to watch Bill, who was playing in the last group with Ben Crenshaw. Although Bill wasn't going to win the individual, the drama at the top of the leaderboard between the Texas twosome was as good as it gets. Tom Kite was in the clubhouse with the lead, and Texas was looking like they would win the team title.

Ben was one shot behind Tom in a fierce battle for the individual title. Bill would eventually finish third. Going to the seventy-second hole, most of the teams were now around the eighteenth to watch. Ben, who had won the previous NCAA individual title, wasn't about to have his childhood rival beat him that week. But it sure looked like that was exactly what was going to happen, especially when Ben got to the tough par-4, eighteenth hole and hit his iron shot forty feet away from the hole.

I mentioned before that Ben was the greatest long putter ever, but could he do it again to tie with Tom for the individual title? Putting up the hill and directly into the Florida grain, Ben smoked his putt. It was definitely too hard, but Ben again shocked the spectators and Tom. It rammed into the back of the hole, jumped six inches straight up, and then went straight back into the hole. Ben had done it again: He sank this forty-foot putt on the seventy-second hole for a last-round 65 to tie with Tom for the individual title. Instead of a playoff, the NCAA declared them cochampions. Tom could only smile and think, *I can't believe he's done this again.* All of us at Houston thought precisely the same thing.

A HUMBLING GAME

Ben had now won the individual title for the second time and would win it again in 1973 for three in a row. The guy was a phenom, plain and simple.

We finished second overall, with Texas on top. Losing to Texas? It felt like getting bucked off a bull at the rodeo in front of your whole family. The NCAA Committee handed us our runner-up trophies, but none of us wanted them. After we went back, showered, and were ready to head back to Houston, our whole team decided to throw our trophies in the garbage. Looking back, I wish I'd kept mine. Second place wasn't so bad, considering the competition, but at the time, it felt like the ultimate failure.

That tournament wasn't only a battle but a preview of greatness. Ben Crenshaw, Tom Kite, Andy North, and Bill Rogers all went on to win major championships, and many others from that field became top PGA Tour players. It was like the golf gods had packed Cape Coral with future legends.

For us, though, it was a tough pill to swallow. Coach didn't come there to finish second, and neither did we. But if there was one thing I learned from that week, it was that, sometimes, even when you give it everything you've got, the other guys are just a little better. And when those other guys are named Ben Crenshaw and Tom Kite, well, there's no shame in that. But don't think for a second we were okay with it—not by a long shot.

From time to time, I still think about the end of 1972. We had such a great team that year, and we were absolutely convinced we would win the NCAA Championship. That confidence wasn't just blind hope. It was based on fact. Just six months earlier, we had won a major college tournament at Cape Coral, Florida, by a staggering twenty-five shots—on the very same course where the NCAA would be held. That kind of dominant victory gave us the belief that no one could beat our team.

Coach believed in us completely. He didn't just say it—he lived it. And we felt it. That belief, coming from a leader like him, is something you don't forget. It bonds a team. It pushes you beyond what you thought possible. It gives you the feeling that you're part of something bigger than yourself.

To be fair, not everything about Coach was textbook inspiration. He had his quirks: his quotes, his speeches, his wild predictions. We used to roll our eyes or laugh under our breath. Some of the guys even said he embarrassed them at times. But, years later, I caught myself repeating those same quotes to my own students. I understood what he was doing. We all did eventually. We learned that inspiration doesn't always come in perfect packaging. Sometimes it's messy, loud, and even awkward—but it stays with you.

That year, we had battled Texas all season long. We'd beaten them more often than not, and we had the firepower to match anyone. But they had two aces—Ben Crenshaw and Tom Kite. That was one of the greatest one-two punches in the history of college golf. In the biggest tournament of the year, they stepped up and took it. They earned it. And as painful as it was for us, we respected it. Over time, those Longhorns we wanted so badly to beat became our friends and competitors we were proud to have gone up against.

I wanted that NCAA title more than anything. I really believed it would change my life—and maybe it would have. But, instead, we came up just short. And in that disappointment, something subtle happened that I didn't fully recognize at the time. That moment—losing the NCAA Championship—may have nudged me down a different path. Not the path of a full-time touring professional, but toward becoming a club professional and eventually a teacher. It quietly changed my direction.

And you know what? It may have been the better path all along.

I'm so grateful now. Grateful for my teammates at the University of Houston. Grateful for the rivalries, the friendships, the lessons. And grateful for Coach Williams, who gave us more than just practice plans and pep talks. He gave us belief.

What a time. What a team. What a true dynasty.

10

CASUALTIES

(Or: The Mass Extinction Event Known as Freshman Year)

Many came in wide-eyed and full of swagger. But make no mistake—many began, and few survived.

Seventeen freshmen entered the fall of 1968 thinking they were going to be the next Ben Hogan. Each had a story, but most didn't make it to 1969. Some left quietly. Others blew out like fireworks. But when the dust settled, they all reached the same conclusion: There just wasn't much hope of ever actually playing golf at the University of Houston.

Enter: Mike Killian — a.k.a. "Killer."

Mike Killian came in hot. He was the top junior golfer in Florida and one of the best in America, and he didn't let anyone forget it. Wiry, fast-talking, and oozing confidence out of every pore, he looked like he believed he was already great. So, naturally, we named him Killer.

The nickname stuck. And to be fair—Killer had game. No question. But what he didn't have was the patience for Coach's long-winded stories, our monster qualifiers, or the endless drives to remote golf courses.

Let me paint a better picture.

We were living four deep in a dorm. On one side of the shared bathroom were me and Bruce Ashworth, a First Team All-American. On the other side were Killer and Jim Simons, a future PGA Tour star. Forty golfers were packed onto one floor. To say there was a lot going on would be a serious understatement. Not to mention that "initiation" began the moment we arrived and didn't end until Christmas break. In addition, Killer did not do particularly well with freshmen initiation such as a plastic golf ball on his head to school or making the Quick Stop runs at night.

Killer and Coach? They were oil and water. Diesel and jet fuel. Killer thought he deserved to be playing immediately, but freshmen weren't eligible for varsity in 1968–69. That didn't matter to Killer—he wasn't buying into the system.

As the first semester ended, he'd had enough. Between Coach's mental warfare, the unforgiving Texas weather, and thirty-nine other guys in Baldwin House, Killer packed up his VW and headed back home. He knew he could transfer to the University of Florida, where they would be was waiting with open arms.

When we returned in January, his bed was empty, and his closet was as bare as his patience. Gone without a trace.

I caught up with Mike years later, and we had a good talk. He told me, "Jim, I never really recovered from Houston. Between Coach Williams and all the hazing . . . it just took the joy out of the game for me."

CASUALTIES

That stuck with me. This guy had big-league talent. But the University of Houston was a crucible—not everyone was built to handle that fire.

He never became the college star everyone expected, but he did eventually make the team for the University of Florida. Killer did rebound and become a very successful club professional—respected and well-liked—and we remain friends to this day.

What I take from the Killer story is that, at the University of Houston, Survival Rate = Not Great.

When I say Houston wasn't for everyone, I mean it. This program chewed guys up and spat them out faster than a jackrabbit on a date.

Seventeen freshmen came in my year. By the end of year one?

Fifteen were gone.

That's not a typo. That's the Coach Williams Way.

It was tough. It was humbling. And it was extremely competitive. But if you could survive Houston, well, you could probably survive anything.

Epilogue

I promised my parents I'd finish college, and I did—returning for one final semester at the University of Houston. By that time, I couldn't play on the golf team, but I roomed with Bill Rogers and Bruce Lietzke and found myself in one last amateur event: the Four States Championship in Texarkana, a tournament long on history. Texas, Oklahoma, Arkansas, and Louisiana. I stayed at Bill's home, played some great golf, and won the tournament. They handed me a trophy the size of Dallas, and it felt like the perfect sendoff.

After graduating in January 1973, with a bachelor's in economics, I stood at a crossroads: remain an amateur and most likely have a Walker Cup spot later that summer, or turn professional. I also had a fabulous job offer in real estate waiting for me in Houston. To solve this issue, I drove out to Champions for a long talk with the wise Jackie Burke. I told him I didn't think I could give up on golf yet. He agreed, and set my mind at ease—my path had already been written in fairways and greens. I'd trained my whole life to play. My amateur record said I was definitely ready for professional golf, and my heart said go.

There was no better place to prepare for life on the PGA Tour than the University of Houston. Coach Williams had

EPILOGUE

built a machine—a dynasty—and we all knew we were part of something rare and special. So, in January, I joined a six-month mini-tour in Los Angeles, the National Golf Tour, with 120 other hungry players. We all put in the up-front ten-thousand-dollar entry fee, and we were off, everyone chasing the same dream: a PGA Tour card at Q-School in the fall.

When I left Houston, I didn't just leave with memories. I left with a brotherhood. The players who made it through those years shared a bond that lasts forever. Whenever I run into anyone who wore the Houston colors, we fall into laughter like no time has passed. The stories, the heat, the grind, the victories—it's all still alive.

Houston toughened me up. I thought I was competitive before I arrived, but I was naive. Houston sharpened me, showing me how great players think, practice, and prepare. I met future PGA Tour legends not just as opponents but as friends, and I met the top players on the top teams from other colleges. This opened the door to my second calling—teaching the game—and I doubt that door would've opened if I hadn't walked through Coach's hallway at Baldwin House.

I learned a tremendous amount about coaching and motivating players from Coach Williams. Even though I didn't realize it so much when I was playing for him, I often thought back to the ideas he presented and the way he motivated us. It definitely had a huge influence on my ability to teach, coach, and motivate much better.

When I left Houston, we had won twelve of the past sixteen NCAA Championships and finished second in the other four. Coach Williams's legacy continued after I left, with the Cougars winning NCAA titles in 1977, 1982, 1985, and 1987.

EPILOGUE

Coach retired at the end of the '87 season with seventeen NCAA Championships—an unmatched record that will likely never be broken.

Looking back, I didn't just attend a university. I joined a dynasty. I became part of a tradition, a story, a team that changed my life.

And for that, I will always be grateful.

www.ingramcontent.com/pod-product-compliance
Lightning Source LLC
LaVergne TN
LVHW030343070526
838199LV00067B/6431